SHAPE IT! 1

T0306625

WORKBOOK

Vicki Anderson and Lynn Durrant

CAMBRIDGE
UNIVERSITY PRESS

CAMBRIDGE
UNIVERSITY PRESS

University Printing House, Cambridge CB2 8BS, United Kingdom

One Liberty Plaza, 20th Floor, New York, NY 10006, USA

477 Williamstown Road, Port Melbourne, VIC 3207, Australia

314–321, 3rd Floor, Plot 3, Splendor Forum, Jasola District Centre, New Delhi – 110025, India

79 Anson Road, #06–04/06, Singapore 079906

Avenida Paulista, 807 conjunto 2315, 01311–915, São Paulo, Brazil

Torre de los Parques, Colonia Tlacoquemécatl del Valle, Mexico City, cp 03200, Mexico

Cambridge University Press is part of the University of Cambridge.

It furthers the University's mission by disseminating knowledge in the pursuit of education, learning and research at the highest international levels of excellence.

www.cambridge.org
Information on this title: www.cambridge.org/9781108810562

First published 2020

20 19 18 17 16 15 14 13 12 11 10 9 8 7 6 5 4 3 2 1

Printed in Great Britain by CPI Group (UK) Ltd, Croydon CR0 4YY

A catalogue record for this publication is available from the British Library

ISBN 978-1-108-81056-2 Shape It! Workbook Level 1
ISBN 978-1-108-71480-8 Own it! Workbook Level 1

Additional resources for this publication at www.cambridge.org/shapeit

CONTENTS

STARTER

Welcome!

VOCABULARY AND READING

Months, Cardinal and Ordinal Numbers, and Colors

1 ☆ **Complete the sentences with the months in the box and ordinal numbers.**

April	August	February	~~January~~
June	March	November	October

1 ___January___ is the first month.
2 ________ is the ________ month.
3 ________ is the third month.
4 ________ is the ________ month.
5 May is the ________ month.
6 ________ is the sixth month.
7 July is the ________ month.
8 ________ is the ________ month.
9 September is the ________ month.
10 ________ is the tenth month.
11 ________ is the ________ month.
12 December is the ________ month.

2 ☆☆ **Complete the crossword with seven more colors.**

ACROSS →
2 three letters
3 four letters
4 six letters
7 five letters
8 five letters

DOWN ↓
1 five letters
5 six letters
6 four letters

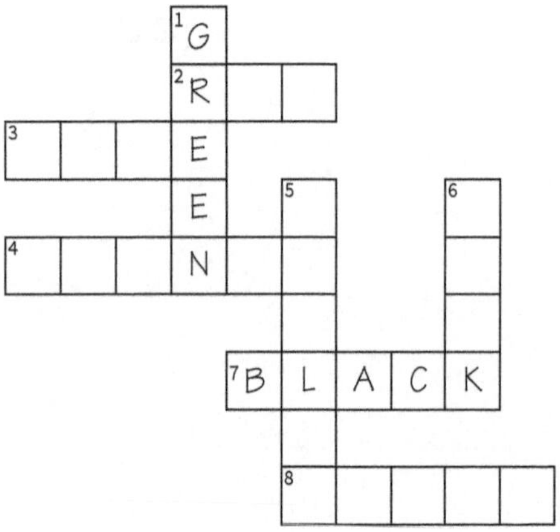

An Online Profile

3 ☆☆ **Read about Dasha and Carlos. Where are their friends from?**

Home | **Profile** | Photos | Events

INTERNATIONAL STUDENT PROFILE DAY!

Hello! My name's Dasha. I'm from Warsaw in Poland. I'm 12. How old are you? In this photo, I'm with my two best friends. Polina is Polish, but Marta isn't Polish. She's Brazilian. My favorite color is green. What's your favorite color?
My birthday is April 10. When's your birthday?
My dream is to be a doctor! What's your dream?
Write soon!

Hi, Dasha! I'm Carlos. I'm Mexican, from Mexico City. I'm 11. In this photo, I'm with my best friends. They're not Mexican. Yusuf is from Turkey, and David is from England. My favorite color is blue. It's June 5 tomorrow, and it's my birthday! My dream is to be a singer! Who's your favorite singer?
Let me know!

4 **Read the profiles again and complete the chart.**

Name	Birthday	Favorite Color	Dream
Dasha	April 10	green	1 ___doctor___
2 ________	3 ________	4 ________	singer

5 ☆☆ **Circle the correct answers.**

1 Dasha is from *China* / *(Poland)*.
2 Her birthday is in the *fourth* / *seventh* month of the year.
3 Carlos is from *Turkey* / *Mexico*.
4 His birthday is in the *sixth* / *twelfth* month of the year.
5 *David* / *Carlos* is 12 tomorrow.

GRAMMAR IN ACTION AND VOCABULARY

Subject Pronouns and Possessive Adjectives

1 ☆ **Complete the chart with the subject pronouns in the box.**

it they we ~~you~~

Singular	Plural
I	3 ________
1 ___you___	you
he / she / 2 ________	4 ________

2 ☆ **Write the subject pronoun.**

1 Dasha ___she___
2 photos ________
3 school ________
4 Carlos ________
5 Polina and Marta ________
6 Yusuf and I ________

3 ☆ **Which plural pronoun can we use for objects and people?**

____

4 ☆ **Complete the sentences with the possessive adjectives in the box.**

her his its my our ~~their~~ your

1 Yusuf and Carlos are at school. They're in ___their___ classroom.
2 He's from Poland. ________ name's Max.
3 I'm 12 years old, and ________ best friend, Alba, is 11.
4 We're from China. ________ nationality is Chinese.
5 You're 13. ________ birthday is in April.
6 My teacher is Maria. ________ birthday is in August.
7 This school is nice. ________ classrooms are big!

Verb *To Be*

5 ☆☆ **Complete the profile with the correct form of *to be*.**

My name [1] ___is___ Sofía. I [2] ________ from Chile. My best friend [3] ________ Ana. She [4] ________ (not) from Chile. She [5] ________ from Brazil. My favorite singer [6] ________ Lorde. My favorite songs [7] ________ *Green Light* and *Royals*. They [8] ________ incredible!

Question Words

6 ☆ **Match questions 1–5 with answers a–e.**

1 Where are you from? [c]
2 How old are you? [ ]
3 When's your birthday? [ ]
4 Who's your best friend? [ ]
5 What's your favorite number? [ ]

a May 10.
b It's 15.
c ~~I'm from Miami.~~
d Alba.
e I'm 11.

Classroom Objects

7 ☆ **Look at the pictures. (Circle) the correct words.**

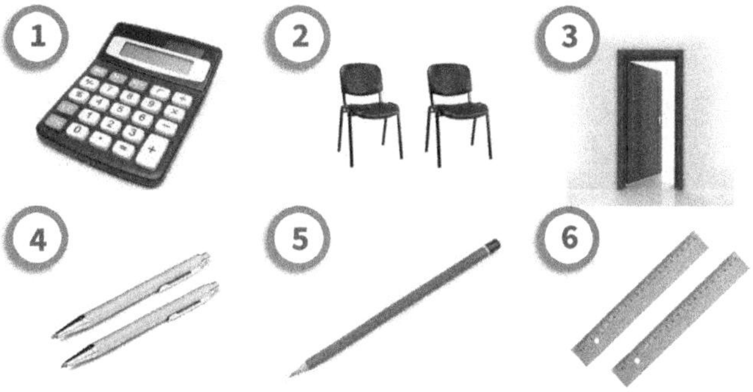

1 It's a *board* / *(calculator)*.
2 They're *chairs* / *desks*.
3 It's a *window* / *door*.
4 They're *pens* / *pencils*.
5 It's a *pen* / *pencil*.
6 They're *rulers* / *notebooks*.

LISTENING AND GRAMMAR IN ACTION

An Introduction

S.01 **1** ☆ **Listen and circle the correct answer.**

Elena's from *Spain* / *Brazil*.

S.01 **2** ☆ **Listen again. Number the instructions in the order you hear them (1–4).**

S.01 **3** ☆☆ **Listen again. Are the sentences *T* (true) or *F* (false)?**

1 This is Elena's first day at school. T

2 She's from the capital of Brazil. ___

3 She's the only student from Brazil in her class. ___

4 Her notebook is on her desk. ___

5 Her pens and pencils are in her bag. ___

6 The ruler on the desk is hers. ___

Whose + Possessive Pronouns

4 ☆☆ **Complete the sentences with the correct possessive pronouns.**

1 Whose dictionaries are these?
They're their dictionaries. They're theirs.

2 Whose ruler is this?
It's my ruler. It's ______________.

3 Whose books are these?
They're our books. They're ______________.

4 Whose poster is that?
It's her poster. It's ______________.

5 Whose chairs are those?
They're your chairs. They're ______________.

6 Whose calculator is this?
It's his calculator. It's ______________.

Imperatives

5 ☆☆ **Put the words in the correct order to make sentences.**

1 write / Don't / notebook / my / in
Don't write in my notebook.

2 board / the / Write / the / words / on
____

3 late / Don't / for / be / class
____

4 teacher / to / Listen / the
____

5 eat / in / class / Don't
____

6 book / your / Close
____

6 ☆☆☆ **Write two more instructions for your class.**

____

____

____

____

____

____

WRITING

An Informal Letter

1 ☆ **Read Jenny's letter. Who is from Australia?**

____

20 Marsh Street
Newark, NJ 07114

October 20

Dear Lucy,

1 My name is Jenny Watts, and I'm 12. I'm from Newark, New Jersey in the United States.

2 My school is great. The classroom is green, orange, and white. It's very nice, with a lot of posters on the walls. Our teacher is friendly, and I'm happy in my new class.

3 My best friend isn't in my class. She goes to a different school. She isn't American like me. She's Australian. Her name is Sarah.

4 My favorite object is my new red and blue notebook. My favorite number is five – my birthday is May 5! My dream is to be a famous singer like you!

Sincerely,

Jenny

2 ☆ **Read the letter again. Match topics a–d with paragraphs 1–4.**

a favorite object, number, birthday, and dream ☐
b name, age, and where she's from [1]
c best friend and nationality ☐
d school and class ☐

3 ☆ **Match phrases 1–3 with functions a–c.**

1 Sincerely, ☐
2 Our teacher is friendly, <u>and</u> I'm happy in my new class. ☐
3 Dear Lucy, ☐

a to start a letter
b to end a letter
c to join two ideas in one sentence

PLAN

4 ☆☆ **Write an informal letter. Decide what information to include in each paragraph. Use the information in Exercise 2 to help you.**

WRITE

5 ☆☆☆ **Write your letter. Remember to include four paragraphs, the address and date, and expressions from the *Useful Language* box (see Student's Book, p9).**

CHECK

6 **Do you ...**
- introduce yourself and give your name, age, and nationality?
- use *and* to join ideas?
- say what your dream is?

1 What is your family like?

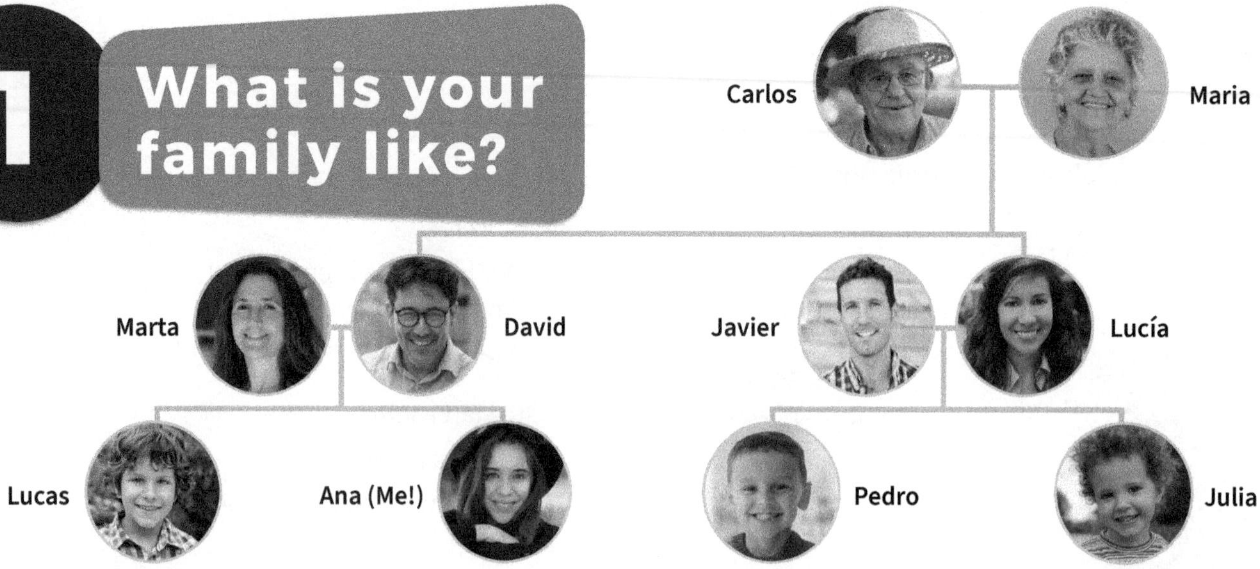

VOCABULARY

Family Members

1 ☆ **Find 14 more words for family in the word search. Look at the words in Exercise 2 to help you.**

W	G	N	E	P	H	E	W	G	S	O	N
(B	R	O	T	H	E	R)	D	F	T	S	E
R	A	D	G	U	J	I	N	K	M	W	K
A	N	U	T	S	S	K	J	I	E	A	Y
V	D	W	H	B	C	U	N	C	L	E	D
G	M	O	M	A	K	E	H	K	M	Y	A
D	A	T	S	N	H	D	A	D	W	D	U
G	R	A	N	D	P	A	E	Q	I	F	G
R	G	U	W	J	O	P	R	T	F	Q	H
B	D	N	I	E	C	E	I	M	E	P	T
F	G	T	K	H	O	S	N	G	X	V	E
C	O	U	S	I	N	S	I	S	T	E	R

2 ☆ **Match 1–8 with a–h to make family word pairs.**

1 brother [f]
2 nephew [ ]
3 husband [ ]
4 grandpa [ ]
5 uncle [ ]
6 dad [ ]
7 son [ ]
8 grandson [ ]

a mom
b wife
c daughter
d aunt
e grandma
f ~~sister~~
g granddaughter
h niece

3 ☆ **Which family word in Exercise 1 can be male or female?** ____________

4 ☆☆ **Look at Ana's family tree. Complete her sentences with the correct family words.**

1 Carlos is my _grandpa_ and María is my ____________.
2 Marta is my ____________ and David is my ____________.
3 Javier is my ____________ and Lucía is my ____________.
4 Lucas is my ____________.
5 Pedro and Julia are my ____________.

5 ☆☆ **(Circle) the correct answer to complete the riddle.**

GUS Hi! I'm Gus, and my sisters are April, May, and June. This is my mom.

MOM Hi! I'm a mom with four children. My daughters are April, May, and June, and this is my son. His name is ________.

a July b September c Gus

Explore It!

Guess the correct answer.

____________ is the most popular boy's name in the United States in the last 100 years.

a Robert b John c James

Find another interesting fact about names. Write a question and send it to a classmate in an email, or ask them in the next class.

READING

A Webpage

1 ☆ **Read the webpage. What is it about? Circle the correct title.**

a A Big Family
b A Small Family
c A Family from Canada

2 ☆☆ **Read the webpage again and <u>underline</u> the words. Then check their meaning and complete the sentences.**

dentist	everyone	fun	~~neighbors~~	whole

1 Your house is next to mine. We're neighbors.
2 My aunt is a ______________. Her job is to look at teeth!
3 A ______________ day is 24 hours long.
4 My favorite day is Sunday with friends and family. It's ______________!
5 This lesson is for all students. It's for ______________.

3 ☆☆ **Read the webpage again. Are the sentences *T* (true) or *F* (false)?**

1 Tom is American. T
2 His mom is a teacher. ___
3 His family is typical because it's big. ___
4 His cousins live on a different street. ___
5 The family is together in the morning and evening. ___
6 Tom is happy at home. ___

4 ☆☆ **Circle the options that are true for you.**

1 My family is *big / small*.
2 My favorite time of day is the *morning / evening*.
3 My neighbors *are / aren't* at my birthday parties.

Tom is from Durham, North Carolina, in the United States. He's seven years old today! His parents' names are Helen and Richard. His mom is a dentist, and his dad is a middle school teacher.

Tom's family isn't very typical. He has two brothers and three sisters, and his grandma and grandpa live with them, too. Tom's aunt, uncle, and four cousins have a house in front of his. The whole family lives on the same street!

Tom's favorite times are the morning and the evening. That's when his family is all together for breakfast and dinner – there are ten people around the table!

Birthdays in Tom's family are fun, too. They have a birthday party every month! Today, everyone is at Tom's party: his family, his friends, and his neighbors.

Is Tom happy in his big family? Yes, he has good friends at school, and a lot of brothers, sisters, and cousins at home!

GRAMMAR IN ACTION

To Have: Affirmative and Negative

1 ☆ **Circle the correct options.**

1 Richard and Helen (*have*) / *has* six children.
2 My grandma *have* / *has* a red car.
3 I *don't* / *doesn't* have a big family.
4 My dad *don't* / *doesn't* have any cousins.
5 My friend's parents *have* / *has* a big house.
6 Uncle Bill *don't* / *doesn't* have any children.

2 ☆☆ **Complete the text with the correct form of *to have*.**

My name is Claudia. I'm from Mexico, but I live in Australia with my family. I [1] ___have___ a big family. I [2] ________ five brothers and two sisters. My parents [3] ________ a big house – it's perfect for a big family! My dad's name is Javier. He [4] ________ a lot of brothers and sisters, too. My mom is named Sandra. She [5] ________ a brother in Mexico – that's my Uncle Sergio. I [6] ________ any aunts or uncles in Australia. They're all in different countries. My best friend, Helen, is Australian. She [7] ________ any brothers or sisters. It's only her! She [8] ________ a small family, but they're really fun! ☺

3 ☆☆ **Write the words in the correct order to make sentences. Then match them with pictures a–e.**

1 bike / I / have / a / don't
I don't have a bike. [b]
2 My / have / grandpa / doesn't / a / cell phone
________ [ ]
3 home / We / pets / at / four / have
________ [ ]
4 best friends / at / school / two / I / have
________ [ ]
5 My / two / has / boards / classroom
________ [ ]

a

b

c

d

e

Possessive *'s*

4 ☆☆ **Complete the sentences with the possessive *'s* and a family word.**

1 My mom *'s mom* is my grandma.
2 My cousin ________ is my uncle.
3 My dad ________ is my uncle.
4 My mom ________ is my aunt.
5 My brother ________ is my mom.
6 My dad ________ is my grandpa.

5 ☆☆☆ **Find four facts about a famous family. Write four sentences about them. Use the correct form of *to have* and the possessive *'s*.**

Angelina Jolie has six children.
____
____
____
____

VOCABULARY AND LISTENING

Describing People

1 ☆ **Complete the list with the words in the box.**

blond	freckles	~~gray~~	tall	wavy

Describing People

Eyes: [1] *gray*, brown

Hairstyle: long, short, [2] ________

Hair color: [3] ________, brown, gray, red

Height: [4] ________, short

Other features: beard, [5] ________, glasses, mustache

2 ☆ **Match the descriptions (1–4) with the photos (a–d).**

1 glasses and long wavy hair
2 long hair and a beard
3 long blond hair
4 short brown hair and glasses

a

b

c

d

A Conversation

1.01 **3** ☆☆ **Listen to the students talking about their families. Write *Paul's family*, *Emma's family*, *Jon's family*, or *Sue's family* under the correct pictures.**

1

____

2

____

3

____

4

____

1.01 **4** ☆☆ **Listen again. Circle the correct answers.**

1 Paul has (*four*) / *five* brothers and sisters.
2 Paul *has* / *doesn't have* blond hair.
3 Emma's sister *has* / *doesn't have* freckles.
4 Emma has a friend with *long* / *short* hair.
5 Jon has *one brother* / *two brothers*.
6 Jon's mom *is* / *isn't* short.
7 Sue has *one tall brother* / *two tall brothers*.
8 *Sue's* / *Tony's* hair is red.

5 ☆☆☆ **Describe a friend. Include information from each category in Exercise 1.**

My friend's name is Cindy. She has brown eyes and long red hair.

GRAMMAR IN ACTION

To Have: Questions

1 ☆ **Complete the chart with *have*, *has*, *do*, *does*, *don't*, or *doesn't*.**

[1] Do you _have_ any cousins?	Yes, I [2]__________.	No, I [3]__________.
[4]__________ they have red hair?	Yes, they [5]__________.	No, they [6]__________.
Does she [7]__________ green eyes?	Yes, she [8]__________.	No, she [9]__________.
How many sisters [10]__________ he have?	He [11]__________ two sisters.	

2 ☆ **Complete the questions with the correct form of *to have*. Then match them with answers a–f.**

1 _Do_ you _have_ any brothers and sisters? [b]
2 __________ your niece __________ brown hair? [ ]
3 __________ you and your family __________ a big house? [ ]
4 __________ your dad __________ a beard? [ ]
5 __________ your parents __________ a car? [ ]
6 __________ your house __________ a lot of rooms? [ ]

a No, he doesn't.
b ~~No, I don't~~.
c Yes, they do.
d Yes, she does.
e Yes, it does.
f No, we don't.

3 ☆☆ **Complete the conversation with the correct form of *to have* and the words in parentheses.**

BETH Hi, Jan. [1] _Do you have_ (you) a lot of homework?
JAN No, I [2]__________.
BETH Good. I have some questions about a school project. [3]____________________ (you) any brothers and sisters?
JAN Yes, I [4]__________. I have two brothers. They're twins.
BETH [5]____________________ (they) green eyes like you?
JAN Yes, they [6]__________!
BETH Cool! And [7]____________________ (your mom) brown hair like you?
JAN No, she [8]__________. She has blond hair.

4 ☆☆☆ **Read the answers from an interview with a famous actor. Write questions with *to have*. Use *How many* when necessary.**

1 _Do you have a big house?_
Yes, I do. My house is very big.
2 ______________________________?
Yes, we have five children, including twins!
3 ______________________________?
We have three boys and two girls.
4 ______________________________?
My wife has a horse, and the children have two rabbits.
5 ______________________________?
Yes, I do. I have two Oscars!

WRITING

An Informal Email

1 ☆ **Look at the photos and read the email. Which photo is of Kylie and Kate? Mark (✓) the correct photo.**

a

b

TO: Ed

FROM: Kate

Hi Ed,

1 How are things? I'm in a new school, and I have a new friend. This email is about her.

2 I have a lot of friends in my class, but one girl [1]*'s* / *'ve* my best friend. Her name [2]*'re* / *'s* Kylie. We say we [3]*'re* / *'ve* twins – we look the same! We have brown hair and green eyes, and we have the same birthday! It [4]*'s* / *'re* funny! 😆 And we both have a little brother. My brother [5]*'re* / *'s* ten and Kylie's brother [6]*'s* / *'re* nine.

3 The photo is of Kylie and me playing basketball. Kylie's a lot of fun and a great friend. 🙂

4 Do you have good friends at your new school? Do you have a best friend? Email me soon!

That's all for now,

Kate

2 ☆☆ **Circle the correct contractions in the email.**

3 ☆☆ **Read the email again. Are the sentences *T* (true) or *F* (false)?**

1 Kate and Kylie are best friends. T
2 They are in different classes. ___
3 Their birthdays are on the same day. ___
4 Kate doesn't have brown hair. ___
5 Kylie doesn't have green eyes. ___
6 They both have a little brother. ___
7 Kate's brother is ten. ___

4 ☆☆ **Match topics a–d with paragraphs 1–4 in the email.**

a extra information about a photo 3
b description of a new friend at school ☐
c introduction and reason for writing ☐
d Kate's questions for Ed ☐

PLAN

5 ☆☆ **Write an informal email to a friend about a new school friend. Make notes about these things:**

your friend's name and age

____

your friend's physical description and family

____

6 **Decide what information to include in each paragraph. Use the information in Exercise 4 to help you.**

WRITE

7 ☆☆☆ **Remember to include four paragraphs, the verbs *to be* and *to have*, and expressions from the *Useful Language* box (see Student's Book, p17).**

CHECK

8 **Do you ...**

- use expressions to start and end your email?
- give information about your friend in the second paragraph?
- use information from a photo in the third paragraph?
- ask questions in the last paragraph?

1 REVIEW

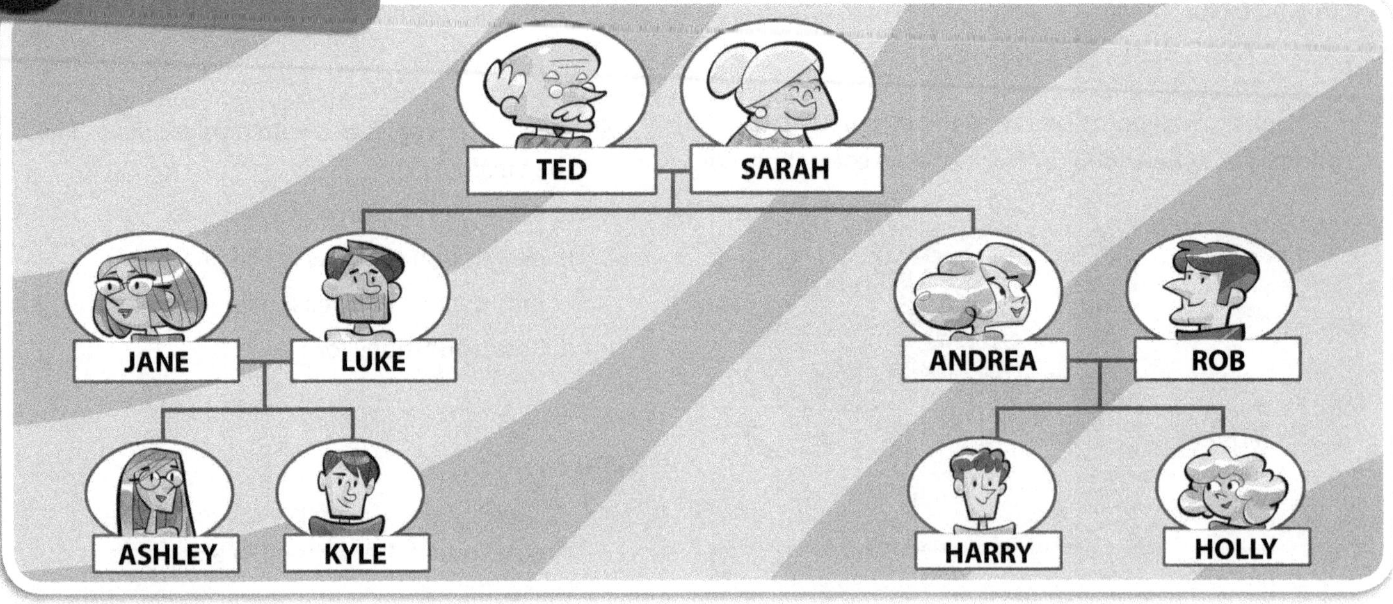

VOCABULARY

1 Look at the family tree. Are the sentences *T* (true) or *F* (false)? Correct the false sentences.

1 Ashley is Kyle's brother. ___
______

2 Jane is Luke's sister. ___
______

3 Ted is Ashley's grandpa. ___
______

4 Luke is Andrea's cousin. ___
______

5 Jane is Kyle's mom. ___
______

6 Luke is Jane's brother. ___
______

7 Kyle and Harry are Ted's grandsons. ___
______

8 Sarah is Luke's and Andrea's grandmother. ___
______

9 Rob is Ashley and Kyle's dad. ___
______

10 Holly is Jane's and Luke's niece. ___
______

2 Circle the word that doesn't fit.

1 mustache / beard / tall
2 wavy / glasses / short
3 blond / freckles / brown
4 blue / green / short
5 long / blond / red
6 brown / tall / wavy

GRAMMAR IN ACTION

3 Circle the correct options.

Victor and Anna [1]*has / have* a big house. It [2]*has / have* a big yard and seven rooms. They [3]*has / have* one daughter named Siena. They [4]*don't have / have* any sons. Anna and Siena [5]*has / have* blond hair. Anna [6]*has / have* blue eyes, and Siena [7]*has / have* brown eyes. Victor [8]*has / have* three sports cars. They're his favorite! Anna [9]*don't have / doesn't have* a sports car, but she [10]*has / have* a mobile home!

4 **Write questions with the correct form of *to have*. Use *How many* when necessary. Then look at Exercise 3 on page 14 and answer the questions.**

1 Victor and Anna / a big yard?

______________________ ______________________

2 rooms / their house?

______________________ ______________________

3 they / sons?

______________________ ______________________

4 Siena / blond hair?

______________________ ______________________

5 sports cars / Victor?

______________________ ______________________

6 Anna / mobile home?

______________________ ______________________

CUMULATIVE GRAMMAR

5 **Match questions 1–8 with answers a–h.**

1 Do your grandparents have a big yard? ☐
2 What do we have for homework? ☐
3 How many cousins do you have? ☐
4 Do you have an English dictionary? ☐
5 Does your dad have a beard? ☐
6 When do we have our exam? ☐
7 Is that Amalia's baby brother? ☐
8 Wow! How many books do your parents have? ☐

a I have four.
b Yes, they do. It's my favorite place!
c I don't know. I think they have hundreds!
d No, he doesn't! But he has a mustache.
e Yes, I do.
f We have the exercises on page 14.
g No! It's her nephew. He's her sister's baby.
h I'm not sure. I think it's in November.

2 What's your day like?

VOCABULARY

Daily Routines

1 ☆ **Complete the crossword. Use the clues.**

ACROSS →

2 You pack your __bag__ with your books for school.

5 I have ______________ with my family. We have cereal.

7 After school, you check your ______________ for messages.

10 In middle school, you do your ______________ every evening.

11 First you wake up. Then you __get up__ .

DOWN ↓

1 I ______________ at seven o'clock, but I get up at 7:15.

3 At night, you ______________ and sleep.

4 In the morning, I __get dressed__ . I put on my school clothes.

5 I ______________ my teeth after breakfast and before I go to bed.

6 After school, I go ______________ on the bus.

8 I go to ______________ from Monday to Friday, but not on the weekend!

9 I take a ______________ when I get up and after sports.

2 ☆ **Complete the daily routines with the verbs in the box.**

brush	check	do	get (x2)	go (x3)	have	pack	take	wake

1 __get__ up
2 ________ dressed
3 ________ my teeth
4 ________ breakfast
5 ________ home
6 ________ my bag
7 ________ to school
8 ________ my phone
9 ________ to bed
10 ________ up
11 ________ a shower
12 ________ my homework

3 ☆☆ **Complete the text with the correct form of the phrases from Exercise 2.**

This is my ideal school day. I [1] __wake up__ at nine o'clock, and I [2] ______________ for messages. I [3] ______________ at 9:15, I take a shower, and I [4] ______________ . These are my favorite clothes. Then I [5] ______________ (cereal). At ten o'clock, I brush my teeth, I [6] ______________ with my books, and I [7] ______________ on the bus. I have three classes, and I go home to have lunch. I don't have any homework! After dinner, I check my phone again and I [8] ______________ .

4 ☆☆☆ **Write about your ideal school day. Use Exercise 3 to help you.**

This is my ideal school day. I …

____

____

____

Explore It!

Guess the correct answer.

People in the United States *get dressed* / *take a shower* in eight minutes.

Find another interesting fact about daily routines in your country. Write a question and send it to a classmate in an email, or ask them in the next class.

READING

A Profile

1 ★ **Read the profile. Is this sentence *T* (true) or *F* (false)?**

Dylan has 25 hours of classes a week. ___

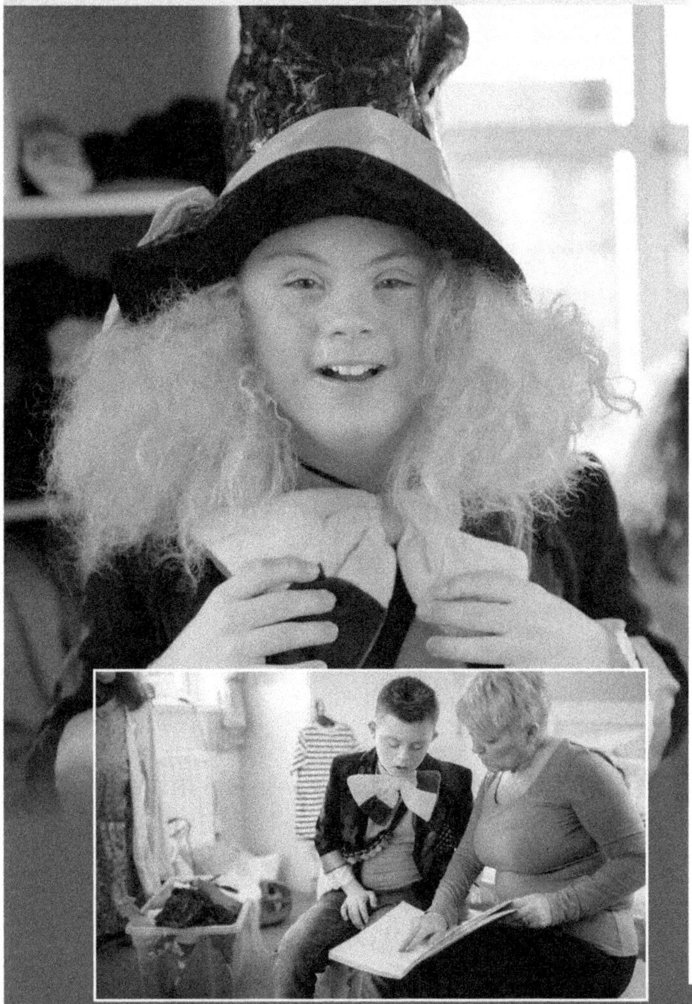

A Day in the Life of a

Child Actor

Dylan Roberts is 14, and he's a child actor. He makes movies and doesn't go to school. He always has classes with special teachers called on-set teachers. Child actors usually have 15 hours of classes a week (schools have 25), but it isn't easy! Dylan often has a lot of work to do.

Dylan talks about his typical day:

"I get up at six in the morning and get dressed. At 6:15, a car takes me to the movie set. I have breakfast at work, and then I practice the day's scenes for an hour. At 8:00, they do my hair and makeup. Filming starts at 9:00. Then, at 11:00, I have a break for half an hour. After that, I go to the teacher's room for classes. I don't have any homework. At 6:00 in the evening, I go home or to a hotel. I take a shower, have dinner, read my part of the movie for tomorrow, and go to bed. It's a busy day!"

2 ★★ **Read the profile again and underline these words. Then check their meaning in a dictionary and complete the sentences.**

break busy filming ~~makeup~~ on-set teacher

1 Here's the green makeup for your eyes.
2 After three classes, we have a ___ to have lunch.
3 All the actors are ready for ___ today.
4 I have an ___ for extra English classes.
5 Our weekends are very ___ with a lot of things to do!

3 ★★ **Read the profile again. Circle the correct answer.**

1 Dylan is a child actor. He *goes* / *doesn't go* to school.
2 Dylan's special teacher is an *on-set teacher*/ *actor*.
3 A child actor *has* / *doesn't have* a lot of work to do.
4 Dylan has breakfast at *home* / *work*.
5 Dylan's first classes are *before* / *after* filming.
6 He doesn't have any *homework* / *breaks*.

4 ★★ **What's your opinion? Read the statements and write *Yes* or *No*.**

1 It's easy to be a child actor. ___
2 Fifteen hours of classes a week is a good idea. ___
3 Dylan's day is fun. ___
4 Not having homework is great. ___

GRAMMAR IN ACTION

Simple Present: Affirmative and Negative

1 ☆ Circle the correct options.

1 Dylan is a child actor and he *make* / *makes* movies.
2 Child actors *don't* / *doesn't* live at home when they are in a movie.
3 They *have* / *has* dinner in a hotel.
4 We *study* / *studies* English.
5 Maya *have* / *has* breakfast at school.
6 On-set teachers *teach* / *teaches* small classes.

2 ☆ Write the third person singular of the simple present.

have	watch	meet	go
1 has	2 ______	3 ______	4 ______

play	brush	do	hurry
5 ______	6 ______	7 ______	8 ______

3 ☆☆ Complete the text with the simple present form of the verbs in parentheses.

Veera is 12. She [1] goes (go) to school in Finland, and her class [2] ______ (have) 18 students. School [3] ______ (start) at 9:45 a.m., and it [4] ______ (end) at 2:45 p.m. There are three or four classes a day. In Finland, students [5] ______ (not have) homework or exams. Veera [6] ______ (have) a lot of free time. After school, she [7] ______ (meet) her friends and they [8] ______ (go) to a sports club for lunch. Veera [9] ______ (love) sports, and she [10] ______ (play) on the school soccer team. Her dream is to be a soccer player!

Adverbs of Frequency

4 ☆ Match the adverbs of frequency with the correct meanings.

1 always [c] a ✓✓
2 usually [ ] b ✗
3 often [ ] c ✓✓✓✓
4 sometimes [ ] d ✓
5 never [ ] e ✓✓✓

5 ☆ Are these statements true for you? Write *T* (true) or *F* (false).

1 I often do my homework with my friends. ___
2 I always check my phone when I wake up. ___
3 My best friend sometimes has lunch at my house. ___
4 I never go to bed late on the weekend. ___
5 I usually have lunch with my grandparents on Sundays. ___

6 ☆☆ Write the words in the correct order to make sentences.

1 makes / dad / often / dinner / My
My dad often makes dinner.
2 I / brush / after / teeth / always / my / breakfast
______
3 go / at / They / lunchtime / usually / home
______
4 sometimes / We / class / are / for / late
______
5 I / check / in / never / my / class / phone
______
6 does / in / the / Dan / park / homework / his / usually
______

VOCABULARY AND LISTENING

Free-Time Activities

1 ☆ Complete the free-time activity phrases.

1 play an ins_t_ _r_ _u_ _m_ent
2 go for a b__ __e r__ __e
3 read a book or a ma__ __ __ __ __e
4 chat on__ __ __e
5 play v__ __ __o g__ __ __s
6 make v__ __ __ __s
7 take ph__ __ __s
8 download s__ __ __s
9 listen to m__ __ __c
10 go sh__ __ __ __ __g
11 hang out with fr__ __ __ __s
12 watch __V

2 ☆☆ Complete the sentences with the correct form of phrases from Exercise 1.

1 Laura often _downloads songs_ from the Internet – she doesn't buy CDs.
2 When I ________________ with my friends, we talk for hours on our computers or phones.
3 I usually meet and ________________ in the park after school.
4 Luke's sister plays the guitar, but he doesn't ________________.
5 I use my phone to ________________ – my friends are the actors. I sometimes put them on YouTube!
6 They never ________________ now. They always find movies and series online.

Street Interviews

2.01 **3 ☆ Listen to the interviews. Circle the correct answer.**

The interviews are about different …

a school activities.
b free-time activities.
c instruments.

2.01 **4 ☆☆ Listen again and number the activities in the photos in the order you hear them (1–3).**

a

b

c

2.01 **5 ☆☆ Listen again and write *A* (Alyssa), *C* (Caleb), or *D* (Destiny).**

1 _A_ does his/her activity every day.
2 ____ and ____ do their activities on the weekend.
3 ____ does his/her activity early in the morning.
4 ____ does his/her activity with animals.
5 ____ uses the Internet for his/her activity.
6 ____ wants to do his/her activity as a job.

6 ☆☆☆ Write about one of your free-time activities. Use the questions below to help you.

Where? How often? When? Who with?

____
____
____
____
____

GRAMMAR IN ACTION

Simple Present: Questions

1 ☆ **Complete the questions with *Do* or *Does*. Then match them with answers a–f.**

1 __Do__ you see your friends on the weekend? [b]
2 ______ your parents like the same music? [ ]
3 ______ your sister watch TV a lot? [ ]
4 ______ your cousin hang out with you? [ ]
5 ______ all your family members play an instrument? [ ]
6 ______ this schedule have ten subjects? [ ]

a No, they don't.
b ~~Yes, I do~~.
c Yes, he does.
d Yes, we do.
e No, she doesn't.
f Yes, it does.

2 ☆☆ **Write the words in the correct order to make questions. Use the photos to help you.**

1 friends / you / online / Do / your / chat / with / ?
Do you chat online with your friends?
2 download / your / Does / best friend / songs / ?
____
3 go / for / Do / you / Sundays / a / bike / ride / on / ?
____
4 shopping / Do / you / go / a lot / ?
____
5 play / games / your / dad / video / Does / ?
____
6 your / books / Does / read / aunt / ?
____

3 ☆☆ **Answer the questions in Exercise 2 for you. Use short answers.**

1 __________ 4 __________
2 __________ 5 __________
3 __________ 6 __________

Wh- Questions

4 ☆ **Circle the correct question words.**

1 *What* / *When* do you do on the weekend?
2 *Where* / *Who* do you go after school?
3 *What* / *Who* does Eric have lunch with?
4 *Where* / *What* do you usually meet Ava?
5 *How often* / *Who* do they go shopping?
6 *Where* / *What time* do you wake up on Mondays?

5 ☆☆ **Read the interview with a tennis player. Complete the questions using the words in parentheses.**

JADE What time [1] __do you get up__ (you / get up), Alina?
ALINA Very early! At six o'clock.
JADE [2] __________ (you / get up) early on weekends, too?
ALINA No, not always.
JADE And how often [3] __________ (you / hang out) with friends?
ALINA I see my friends twice a week.
JADE [4] __________ (your friends / come) to your matches?
ALINA Yes, sometimes they do.
JADE Great! And [5] __________ (your parents / watch) you, too?
ALINA Yes. My dad comes to all my matches.
JADE Nice! And [6] __________ (other people / ask) you to do interviews?
ALINA No, they don't! I'm not famous!

WRITING

An Article

1 ☆ **Read the article. Circle the correct title.**

a What does Zev do on the weekend?

b What is Zev's daily routine?

Zev is an American student. He's 12 years old. In his free time, he's a photographer. Zev's photos are of animals and objects. He often makes photo stories. He uses digital technology and his imagination.

1 This is a typical day in Zev's life. He always gets up at 7:00 and takes a shower. At 7:30, he has breakfast. At 7:45, he brushes his teeth and packs his bag. He then goes to school at 8:00.

2 In the afternoon, Zev goes home. At 3:00, he usually has lunch and does his homework. He goes for a walk with his sister at 5:00 and looks for ideas for his photo stories.

3 From 6:30 to 8:00 in the evening, Zev makes his photo stories and puts them on his website. He sometimes chats online with his friends, but he never stays up late. At 9:30, Zev goes to bed.

One day, I want to take photos like Zev!

2 Match topics a–c with paragraphs 1–3.

a description of Zev's evening routine ☐

b description of his morning routine ☐

c description of his afternoon routine ☐

3 ☆ **Read the article again. What time does Zev do these things?**

1 gets up *7:00*

2 has breakfast ________

3 packs his bag ________

4 goes to school ________

5 has lunch ________

6 goes for a walk ________

7 makes his photo stories ________

8 goes to bed ________

4 ☆ **Find and underline five adverbs of frequency in the article.**

5 ☆☆ **Rewrite the sentences with the correct punctuation.**

1 how does Zev make his photo stories

How does Zev make his photo stories?

2 zevs sister doesnt take photos

____

3 zevs friends look at his photo stories

____

4 wow I think the photos are great

____

PLAN

6 ☆☆ **Write an article about someone's day. Choose a person with a different daily routine than yours. It can be a friend or someone from your family. Decide what information to include in each paragraph. Use the information in Exercise 2 to help you.**

WRITE

7 ☆☆☆ **Write your article. Remember to include the information in the correct order, the simple present, adverbs of frequency, and correct punctuation from the *Useful Language* box (see Student's Book, p29).**

CHECK

8 Do you …

- include an interesting title with a question?
- introduce the person, their nationality, and what they do?
- describe the person's morning, afternoon, and evening routines?
- end the article with a sentence about you and your ambition?

2 REVIEW

VOCABULARY

1 Complete the text with the words in the box.

brush do dressed get go (x2) have pack shower up

I wake [1]__________ at 6:30, and I [2]__________ up at 7:00. Then I take a [3]__________ and [4]__________ my teeth. I get [5]__________ and [6]__________ my bag for school. At 7:30, I [7]__________ breakfast with my mom and dad. I [8]__________ to school at 8:30 and finish at 3:30. In the afternoon, I [9]__________ my homework, and then I have some free time. In the evening, I have dinner with my parents, and then I [10]__________ to bed at about 10:00.

2 Match the verbs with the activities.

1 chat	☐	a songs
2 download	☐	b a bike ride
3 go for	☐	c online
4 listen to	☐	d a book or a magazine
5 hang out with	☐	e music
6 read	☐	f friends
7 go	☐	g TV
8 watch	☐	h shopping

GRAMMAR IN ACTION

3 Complete the sentences with the simple present form of the verbs in parentheses.

1 I __________ (not wake up) early on the weekend.
2 Martin __________ (go) to school at 9:00 every day.
3 We __________ (not do) our homework at school.
4 Tom's dad __________ (make) videos of his birthday every year.
5 Isabela __________ (not have) a big breakfast, only fruit.
6 Theo __________ (not play) the guitar very often.

4 Complete the sentences with the missing words. Circle the correct options.

1 Daniel __________ shopping with his mom.
a sometimes goes b goes sometimes
2 I __________ video games with my brother.
a play often b often play
3 My dad __________ to rock music!
a listens never b never listens
4 We __________ with friends on the weekend.
a always hang out b hang out always
5 They finish their homework, and they __________ TV.
a watch often b often watch

5 **Complete the questions and answers with the simple present form of the verbs in parentheses. Add *Wh-* question words where necessary.**

1 **A:** ________ you ________ (brush) your teeth every day? **B:** Yes, I ________.
2 **A:** ________ your mom ________ (pack) your bag for you? **B:** No, she ________.
3 **A:** ________ your cousins ________ (play) an instrument? **B:** No, they ________.
4 **A:** ________ time ________ Chris ________ (go) home? **B:** At 7:00.
5 **A:** ________ often ________ you ________ (read) a book? **B:** Every month.
6 **A:** ________ ________ you ________ (go) on Sundays? **B:** I often go to the park with my family.

CUMULATIVE GRAMMAR

6 **Complete the conversation with the missing words. Circle the correct options.**

ROSA 1 ________ do you do in your free time?
MIRA I 2 ________ my best friend or go with my brother for a bike ride.
ROSA 3 ________ you see your best friend every day?
MIRA Yes, most days. 4 ________'s your best friend?
ROSA That's Susan, but I 5 ________ her all the time.
MIRA 6 ________ often do you see her?
ROSA It depends, but usually every weekend. We sometimes 7 ________ basketball on Saturdays.
MIRA Hey! I play, too. What 8 ________ do you meet on Saturdays?
ROSA Usually in the afternoon.
MIRA 9 ________ to hang out one Saturday?
ROSA Sure! 10 ________ your phone? Here's my number.
MIRA Yes, I 11 ________. OK, great!

1 a What b Where
2 a meet usually b usually meet
3 a Does b Do
4 a Who b When
5 a don't see b doesn't see
6 a When b How
7 a play b plays
8 a often b time
9 a You want b Do you want
10 a Have do you b Do you have
11 a do b do have

3 How do we learn?

VOCABULARY

School Subjects

1 ☆ **Complete the subjects with the correct letters.**

1 Eng_l_ish
2 Spani_h
3 vocatio_al educati_n
4 m_th
5 musi_
6 ar_
7 d_ama
8 geo_raphy
9 histor_
10 nut_ition
11 P_
12 sci_nce
13 I_

2 ☆ **Write the correct school subjects from Exercise 1.**

1 ___music___

5 ________

2 ________

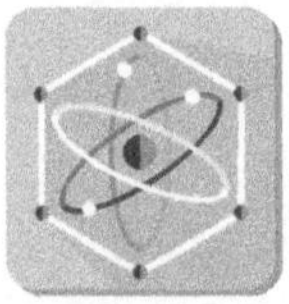

6 ________

3 ________

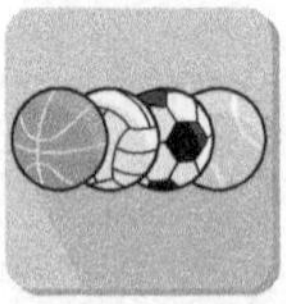

7 ________

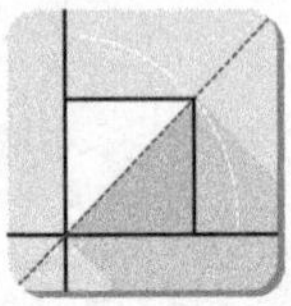

4 ________

8 ________

3 ☆☆ **Write the subjects for the definitions.**

1 You learn to play an instrument. ___music___
2 You learn a language that people speak in a lot of countries in South America. ________
3 You learn about people, countries, and places. ________
4 You learn about things in the past. ________
5 You learn about numbers, shapes, and space. ________
6 You learn a language that people speak in the UK and the United States. ________
7 You learn about food and what is good or bad to eat. ________
8 You do experiments. ________

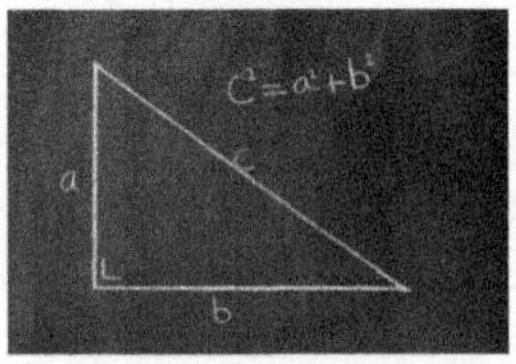

4 ☆☆ **Write the names of these subjects in your language. Write *S* if they are similar to the words in English, or *D* if they are different.**

1 science ________ __
2 geography ________ __
3 drama ________ __
4 art ________ __

Explore It!

Guess the correct answer.

One school in Lucknow, India, has a lot of students. How many students does it have?

a about 15,000 b about 27,000 c about 52,000

Find another interesting fact about school subjects in another country. Write a question and send it to a classmate in an email, or ask them in the next class.

READING

A Webpage

1 ☆ **Read the webpage about schools in Singapore. Why don't teachers like posters in math classrooms?**

____

HOME | STORIES | PHOTOS

SCHOOLS IN SINGAPORE

STUDENTS FROM SINGAPORE OFTEN GET VERY GOOD SCORES IN MATH AND SCIENCE ON INTERNATIONAL TESTS.

In math classes, students can use technology to answer the different math problems. Their answers go on the whiteboard at the front of the class. All students can see and talk about their classmates' answers.

A lot of math classrooms don't have posters on the walls. Teachers don't think posters help students learn.

Students can't talk to each other a lot. They work alone, but they can ask the teacher questions when they don't understand something.

In science classes, students can work on their projects once a week. In one class, they can build a robotic arm, and in another class, students can make a small radio.

In many high schools in Singapore, students don't do a lot of drama, language, music, or art. Some teachers say, "Art subjects aren't very important. Students need to be good at science and math. They need these subjects for their adult life."

Is this a good or a bad idea? What do you think?

2 ☆☆ **Read the webpage again and <u>underline</u> these words. Then check their meaning in a dictionary and complete the sentences.**

~~adult~~	alone	build
scores	whiteboard	

1 In many countries, you're an *adult* when you're 18.

2 My teacher always writes the answers on the ______.

3 I never get good ______ on geography tests. Maps are difficult!

4 We want to ______ a robot for our project.

5 **A:** Do you need help?

B: No, thanks. I always do my homework ______.

3 ☆☆ **Answer the questions.**

1 What subjects are students from Singapore often good at?

math and science

2 What do teachers show on the whiteboard?

____

3 How do students work in math classes?

____

4 How often do students work on science projects?

____

5 Which subjects are not very important in many schools?

____

4 ☆☆☆ **Answer the questions with your own ideas.**

1 "Art subjects aren't very important." What do you think?

____

2 Which subjects do you think are important? Why?

____

GRAMMAR IN ACTION

Can for Ability and Permission

1 ☆ (Circle) the options that are true for you.

1 In our classes, we *can* / *can't* put posters on the walls.
2 At break time, we *can* / *can't* play and talk to friends.
3 We *can* / *can't* talk in science classes.
4 We *can* / *can't* build interesting things for our projects.
5 Sometimes we *can* / *can't* work in groups in our English classes.

2 ☆☆ Complete the sentences. Use *can/can't* and the verbs in parentheses.

1 My dad __can't sing__ because he doesn't have a good voice, but he ________ amazing pictures. (sing / draw)
2 My cousin ________ good photos, but she ________ videos. She's really bad at it! (take / make)
3 My mom ________ salsa very well, and she ________ the guitar, too. She's really good at it! (dance / play)
4 My little brother's four. He ________ English very well, but he ________ it. (speak / read)

3 ☆☆ Complete the texts with *can/can't* and the verbs in parentheses.

My favorite subject is history. I like it because we [1] __can work__ (work) in groups – it's great when we [2] ________ (do) projects together. But we work alone when we have an exam – we [3] ________ (talk). After the exam, we usually take a break, and we [4] ________ (hang out) with friends.

My favorite teacher is Mr. Bell, our geography teacher. I like his classes because we [5] ________ (ask) questions when we need to. We have options, too: sometimes we [6] ________ (choose) our homework, and we [7] ________ (bring) interesting things to class. But we [8] ________ (be) late – Mr. Bell doesn't like that!

4 ☆☆ Write questions and short answers with *can*.

1 students / check their phone / in class? (✗)
Can students check their phone in class?
No, they can't.
2 students / ask questions / in class? (✓)
____
____
3 Kate / play the piano? (✓)
____
____
4 María / speak two languages? (✗)
____
____
5 students / work in groups / in math classes? (✓)
____
____
6 he / do ballet? (✗)
____
____

5 ☆☆ Are these statements true for you? Write *T* (true) or *F* (false).

1 I can speak two languages. __
2 I can dance salsa. __
3 I can ride a bike. __
4 I can play the guitar. __
5 I can sing. __

VOCABULARY AND LISTENING

Places in a School

1 ☆ **Read the definitions. Then circle the correct places in the spidergram.**

1 You can do outdoor sports here.
2 You can buy and eat food here.
3 You can do PE here.
4 Teachers can plan their lessons here.
5 You can leave your bag here.
6 You can read books and study here.
7 You can wash your hands here.

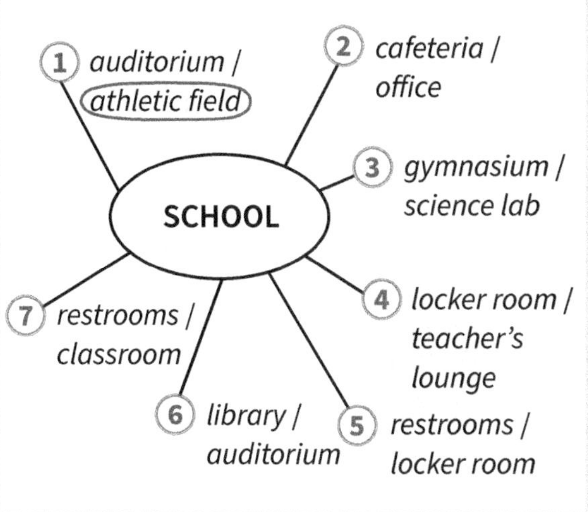

2 ☆☆ **Complete the text with places from Exercise 1.**

Mondays!

I don't like my schedule on Mondays! At 8:45, I go to the [1] *office* and say hello to my aunt – she works at the school. Then I go to the [2] ______________ and put my sports shoes in my locker. After that, my class goes to the [3] ______________ and we do experiments. I don't like science! At break time, I usually go to the [4] ______________ for some food. Then we have PE in the [5] ______________ and then lunch. In the afternoon, it's music and drama. At 4:15, we go to the [6] ______________ and get a book to read – that's OK because I like books, but I'm always happy on Mondays at 4:30 because I can go home!

A Radio Program

3.01 **3** ☆☆ **Listen and number the places in the order you hear them (1–6).**

a 
auditorium

b 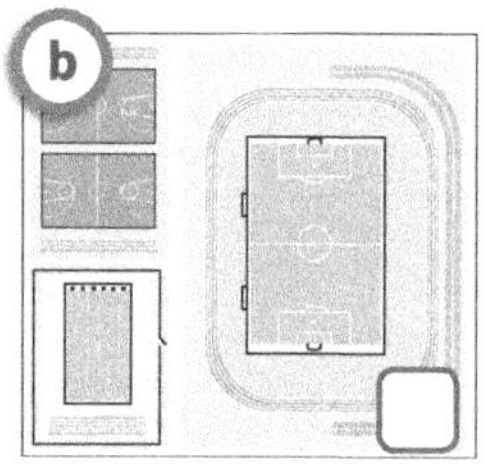
athletic field

c 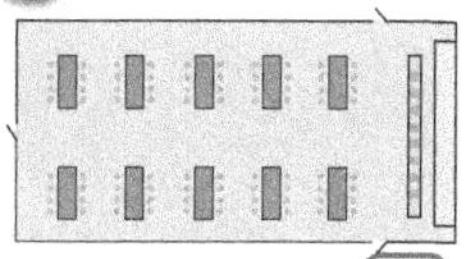
cafeteria

d 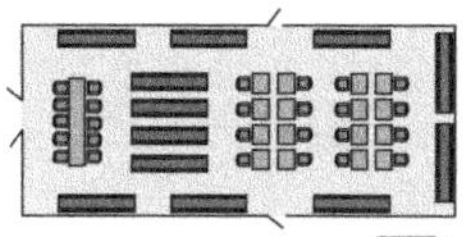
library

e 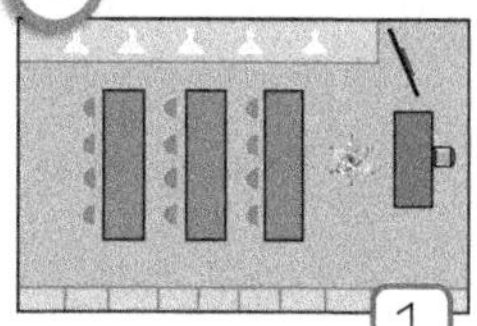 1
science lab

f 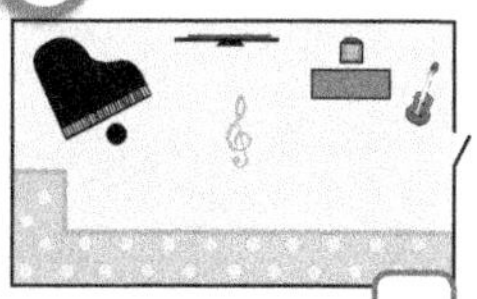
music classroom

3.01 **4** ☆☆ **Listen again. Are the sentences *T* (true) or *F* (false)?**

1 Alex likes the science lab. *T*
2 He likes the magazines from the library. ____
3 Alex's favorite subject is PE. ____
4 The music classroom is Alex's favorite place. ____
5 Marina has lunch in the cafeteria. ____
6 She likes all the places in the school. ____

GRAMMAR IN ACTION

Verb Forms: (*Don't*) *Like*, *Don't Mind*, *Love*, *Hate* + *-ing*

1 ☆ **Match the verbs with the emojis.**

1 love [b] 2 like [ ] 3 don't mind [ ]
4 don't like [ ] 5 hate [ ]

a  b  c  d  e 

2 ☆☆ **Write sentences with the correct form of the verbs.**

1 I / like / go / to the music club
I like going to the music club.
2 We / hate / have / a lot of homework
____
3 Tariq / not mind / play / sports in the gymnasium
____
4 Gina / love / play / soccer / on the athletic field
____
5 They / not like / learn / history
____

3 ☆☆ **Complete the text with the correct form of the verbs in parentheses.**

I have a twin brother, but we're very different! He [1] *hates getting up* (hate / get up) early, but I [2] ________ (not mind / do) it for school. He [3] ________ (love / play) sports, and I [4] ________ (like / play) video games. I [5] ________ (not like / go) to parties. I [6] ________ (like / stay) at home. My brother [7] ________ (love / hang out) with his friends and [8] ________ (have) a good time. He [9] ________ (not mind / study) sometimes, but he doesn't love it. I [10] ________ (love / learn) new things, especially about science.

Object Pronouns

4 ☆ **Complete the chart with the object pronouns.**

Subject	I	you	he	she	it	we	they
Object	1 *me*	2 ____	3 ____	4 ____	5 ____	6 ____	7 ____

5 ☆ **Circle the correct option.**

1 **A:** Do you like drama? **B:** Yes, I like (*it*) / *them*.
2 Mr. Patel isn't in the office. Can you call *her* / *him*?
3 I have a problem. Can you help *me* / *it*, please?
4 Is Amaya here? I can't see *you* / *her*.
5 **A:** Do you like video games? **B:** I hate *it* / *them*.
6 What classes do we have today? Can you give *us* / *you* the schedule, please?

6 ☆☆ **Look at the pictures and then complete the text with the correct subject or object pronouns.**

Me (Josh)

Lucas

Lucas' mom

Spanish

I'm Josh, and Lucas is my best friend. [1] *We* (Josh + Lucas) 're in the same class and [2] ________ (Lucas) lives near [3] ________ (Josh). Lucas' mom is Spanish. [4] ________ (Lucas' mom) speaks Spanish with [5] ________ (Lucas) at home, but [6] ________ (Josh) speak English with [7] ________ (Lucas + Lucas' mom). We learn Spanish at school, and Lucas helps [8] ________ (Josh) with my homework. Spanish is difficult, but I like [9] ________ (¡HOLA!).

WRITING

A Description

1 ☆ **Read Sanjiv's description. Does he like his school?**

____

My School

[1] Tracks and Subjects

I study at a very big school. Students can take different tracks, <u>such as</u> science or arts. I'm on the science track. I study English, math, and science, and technology subjects, <u>like</u> computer science. That's my favorite subject.

[2] ______________________

I really like the teachers. They teach regular classes, but they also teach some after-school clubs, <u>like</u> astronomy and dance. I like being with my teachers after class.

[3] ______________________

We have six classes a day and homework. I don't mind doing some homework, but I don't like a lot of it! I really like working with my classmates on group projects. I don't like working alone!

[4] ______________________

Our school has great places for classes and activities. <u>For example</u>, we have a big gymnasium, a cafeteria, a computer lab, and three science labs. I love studying here.

2 ☆ **Write the correct heading for each paragraph in the description.**

Great Teachers ~~Tracks and Subjects~~
School Places School Routine

3 ☆ **Read the description again. Then complete the text below with the phrases in the box.**

computer science	doing a lot of homework
~~the teachers at his school~~	working alone

Sanjiv likes [1] *the teachers at his school* and [2] ______________________. He doesn't like [3] ______________________ or [4] ______________________.

4 ☆ **Look at the <u>underlined</u> words and phrases in Sanjiv's description. What does he use them for? (Circle) the correct answer.**

a to join ideas
b to show different times
c to give examples

PLAN

5 ☆☆ **Write a description of your school. Make a spidergram of your school in your notebook and use the plan below.**

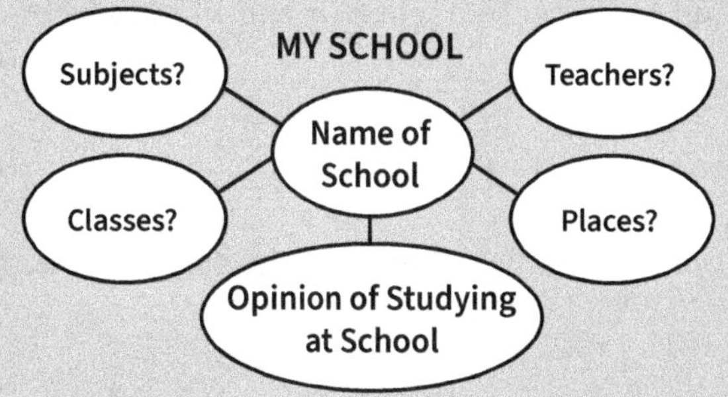

6 **Decide what information to include in each paragraph. Use your spidergram and the information in Exercise 2 to help you.**

WRITE

7 ☆☆☆ **Write your description. Remember to include four paragraphs, *can/can't,* and expressions from the *Useful Language* box (see Student's Book, p41).**

CHECK

8 **Do you ...**

- give the name of the school in the opening sentence?
- include all of the information from your spidergram?
- give your opinion about studying at the school in your closing sentence?

3 REVIEW

VOCABULARY

1 Complete the school subjects.

1 Languages: E______, S______
2 Numbers: m___
3 The past: h______
4 Countries: g________
5 In a lab: s______
6 Art subjects: d_____, m_____, a__
7 Sports: p________ e_________
8 IT: i___________ t__________
9 Food: n_________

2 Find 12 places in a school in the word search.

O	L	H	W	L	I	B	R	A	R	Y	P	S	O
T	E	A	C	H	E	R	S	L	O	U	N	G	E
C	Y	C	A	F	E	T	E	R	I	A	I	U	T
L	O	C	K	E	R	R	O	O	M	E	G	M	W
A	Z	G	Y	M	N	A	S	I	U	M	F	R	P
S	A	T	H	L	E	T	I	C	F	I	E	L	D
S	P	A	U	D	I	T	O	R	I	U	M	T	W
R	S	C	I	E	N	C	E	L	A	B	A	B	T
O	O	H	O	P	R	E	S	T	R	O	O	M	S
O	C	T	B	G	N	G	T	O	F	F	I	C	E
M	W	B	U	F	T	A	P	F	Y	E	I	D	B
C	O	M	P	U	T	E	R	L	A	B	N	F	T

GRAMMAR IN ACTION

3 Look at the chart. Complete the sentences with *can/can't* and the correct verbs.

 Jon	✓	✗	✓
 Lisa	✗	✓	✓

1 Jon ______________ the guitar.
2 Lisa ______________ the guitar.
3 ______________ Jon ______________ songs in English? ______________, he ______________.
4 ______________ Lisa ______________ songs in English? ______________, she ______________.
5 Jon and Lisa ______________ Spanish.

4 Look at the symbols. Write sentences using (*don't*) *like*, *don't mind*, *love*, *hate* + *-ing*.

1 We / 😀 / talk to / our teachers ______________________
2 I / 🙁 / do / homework ______________________
3 She / 😍 / listen / to music ______________________
4 They / 😐 / have / lunch at school ______________________
5 He / 😠 / be / late for class ______________________

5 Match questions 1–6 with answers a–f.

1 Does Tom like soccer? ☐
2 Does Beth play video games? ☐
3 Can you help Suzi? ☐
4 Is Harry in your class? ☐
5 Is this party for you and your friends? ☐
6 Do you like reading? ☐

a No, it isn't for us!
b No, he hates it!
c I don't mind it.
d Yes, she loves them.
e Yes, I can help her.
f Yes, he is.

CUMULATIVE GRAMMAR

6 Complete the conversation with the missing words. Circle the correct options.

DENIZ Hi, Kate! [1] ________ soccer today?
KATE No, I [2] ________ . It's Wednesday today.
DENIZ When [3] ________ practice?
KATE On Tuesdays and Thursdays, and on the weekend [4] ________ have games.
DENIZ Oh! And [5] ________ your parents watch your games?
KATE It depends. [6] ________ come and see me.
DENIZ Hey, [7] ________ do we finish school today?
KATE At three o'clock! It's Wednesday, remember?
DENIZ Oh, great! Harry and I [8] ________ for a bike ride after school on Wednesdays.
KATE [9] ________ Harry now?
DENIZ He's in the library. He [10] ________ a math project to finish.
KATE Well, I love [11] ________ my bike. [12] ________ I go with you?
DENIZ Sure!

	a	b	c
1	Do you have	Have you	You have
2	doesn't	don't have	don't
3	do you have	have you	you have
4	always we	we always	it always
5	does	do	are
6	They sometimes	Them sometimes	Sometimes them
7	when	who	what
8	go usually	usually goes	usually go
9	What's	Where's	Who's
10	has	have	don't have
11	riding	ride	rides
12	Do	Can	Have

4 What do you like to eat?

VOCABULARY

Food and Drink

1 ☆ **Complete the chart with the words in the box.**

~~apples~~ bananas cheese chicken eggs fish juice rice soda

Food from Plants	Food from Animals	Drinks
apples	______	______
______	______	______
______	______	
	______	

2 ☆☆ **Circle the correct answers in the quiz.**

ALL ABOUT FOOD AND DRINK

1 Which food is NOT usually a cake?
a chicken **b** chocolate

2 Which of these is NOT protein?
a meat **b** carrots

3 Which of these is NOT from fruit?
a juice **b** chocolate

4 Which of these is NOT from a plant?
a meat **b** rice

3 ☆☆ **Complete the food words in the text.**

I'm Zara from Malaysia. I usually have kaya toast with [1]e g g s for breakfast. I have lunch at school. Lunch is usually rice and [2]me_ _ or [3]ch_ _ _ _ _ curry with vegetables. I drink [4]ju_ _ _ made from oranges and purple [5]ca_ _ _ _ _ and red [6]ap_ _ _ _. It's yummy! My mom cooks dinner. I love her [7]fi_ _ curry with [8]be_ _ _. We always drink [9]w_ _ _ _.

4 ☆☆☆ **What is your favorite food for breakfast, lunch, and dinner? Write about what you eat. Use Exercise 3 to help you.**

I usually have ...

______

______

______

Explore It!

Guess the correct answer.

Which country grows millions of bananas?

a the United States
b Ecuador
c China

Find another interesting fact about food in your country. Write a question and send it to a classmate in an email, or ask them in the next class.

READING

An Article

1 ☆ **Read the article and match the foods in the box with the photos (1–3).**

blinis	herring with potatoes	mooncakes

Welcome to My Festival!

1 ______

2 ______

3 ______

Hugo:
Midsummer Eve, Sweden

I love this festival in June. It's at the beginning of summer vacation. We go to the country, and in the morning, we get some flowers for our hair. Then we dance to traditional music. Lunch is outside, and it's big! We always eat herring (a type of fish) with potatoes. Later, people play instruments and dance all night!

Mei Lin:
Moon Festival, China

My favorite festival is in September, when we can see the first full moon of the month. We make paper lights and go to the park. And of course, we eat a mooncake or two! These are small round cakes (like the moon!) that have different fillings. I like the chocolate one. We give them to our friends and eat them together.

Daria:
Maslenitsa Pancake Festival, Russia

This great festival is in February. We have fun activities for seven days! We do some sports, play music, dance, and eat a lot of food. I love having blinis. They are Russian pancakes made with butter, eggs, and milk. We eat them with different toppings. My favorite topping is salmon and cream cheese. Yummy!

2 ☆☆ **Read the article again and underline these words. Then check their meaning in a dictionary and complete the sentences.**

country	fillings	full moon	pancakes	~~toppings~~

1 What are your favorite *toppings* on a pizza? I love extra cheese!

2 Every four weeks, we can see the ______ in the sky. It's completely round.

3 *Empanadas* are popular in South America. They have different ______ inside, such as meat or vegetables.

4 I love going to the ______ and looking at the trees and flowers.

5 We need milk and butter to make ______.

3 ☆☆ **Read the article again and complete the chart.**

Festival	Country	Month	Special Food
Midsummer Eve	Sweden	1 *June*	2 ______
Moon Festival	3 ______	4 ______	mooncakes
Maslenitsa	5 ______	February	6 ______

4 ☆☆☆ **Answer the questions with your own ideas.**

1 Which of the festivals is your favorite? Why?

______

2 Think of a festival in your country. When is it? What food do you have?

______

GRAMMAR IN ACTION

Countable and Uncountable Nouns

1 ☆ **Write the correct headings in the chart: *Countable* or *Uncountable*.**

1 ______	2 ______
cheese water bread rice ______ ______	apple egg tomato ______ ______ ______

2 ☆ **Complete the chart in Exercise 1 with the words in the box.**

bean carrot chocolate fish ~~rice~~ taco

A/An, Some/Any

3 ☆ **Circle the correct options.**

1 We use *a* or *an* with *countable* / *uncountable* nouns.
2 We use *some* and *any* with *singular* / *plural* countable nouns and uncountable nouns.
3 We use *some* in *affirmative* / *negative* sentences.
4 We use *any* in *affirmative* / *negative* sentences and questions.

4 ☆☆ **Complete the sentences with the words in the box.**

~~apple~~ chocolate eggs juice sandwich

1 Do you have apple for your snack?
2 We don't have any ______ for an omelet.
3 I'm hungry. Do you have a ______ for me?
4 Drink some ______ with your breakfast.
5 Can we have some ______ after dinner?

5 ☆☆ **Complete the conversation with *a*, *an*, *some*, or *any*.**

KIM What can we have for dinner? Do we have [1] any rice?
DAN No, we don't have [2] ______ rice, but we have [3] ______ pasta.
KIM Pasta with cheese! Do we have [4] ______ cheese?
DAN No. I can see [5] ______ tomato and [6] ______ egg, but that's all! Let's go to the store.
KIM OK. Can you write a list? We need [7] ______ cheese, [8] ______ milk, and [9] ______ tomatoes. Is that all?
DAN No. We don't have [10] ______ drinks. We need [11] ______ juice.
KIM Right! And [12] ______ chocolate!

6 ☆☆☆ **What is your favorite dinner? What do you have at home to make it and what do you need? Write sentences with *a*, *an*, *some*, and *any*.**

I want ______ for dinner.
I have ______
I don't have ______
I need ______

VOCABULARY AND LISTENING

Adjectives

1 ★ Complete the adjectives with the missing vowels. Then match adjectives 1, 5, 7, and 10 with the photos (a–d).

1 h o t [d]
2 d _ l _ c _ _ _ s
3 _ nh _ _ lthy
4 d _ sg _ st _ ng
5 sw _ _ t [ ]
6 sp _ cy
7 c _ ld [ ]
8 h _ _ lthy
9 fr _ sh
10 s _ lty [ ]

a

b

c

d

2 ★★ Circle the correct options.

1 Careful! The milk is *cold* / *hot* !
2 I don't like beans. They're *delicious* / *disgusting*!
3 Ice cream is perfect for a hot day. It's *hot* / *cold* and *sweet* / *spicy*.
4 Water is a *healthy* / *unhealthy* drink, but soda is *healthy* / *unhealthy*.
5 I like having *disgusting* / *fresh* fruit for breakfast.

A Quiz

4.01 3 ★ Listen to the family. Do they answer all the questions in the quiz?

____

4.01 4 ★ Listen again. Match the foods (1–3) with the restaurants (a–c).

1

kebab

2

taco

3

curry

a La Cantina b Kumkapi c Bangkok Garden

4.01 5 ★★ Listen again. Are the sentences *T* (true) or *F* (false)?

1 The restaurants in the quiz are new. T
2 The names of the restaurants are in the first question. ___
3 The girl thinks Turkish food is sweet. ___
4 "Fresh" and "healthy" describe two of the three types of food. ___
5 The boy thinks kebabs are delicious. ___
6 The children both want to go to the Mexican restaurant. ___

6 ★★★ Do you prefer Mexican, Turkish, or Thai food? Look on the Internet for more information about these types of food. Write your ideas.

I prefer ______________ food because it's ______________

____

____

____

GRAMMAR IN ACTION

There Is/Isn't, There Are/Aren't

1 ★ **Look at the picture of the restaurant. Circle the correct options.**

1 There is / *isn't* a picture on the wall.
2 There *is some* / *isn't any* water in the glasses.
3 There *is some* / *isn't any* food on the tables.
4 There *are some* / *aren't any* children.
5 There *are* / *aren't* eight people.
6 There *is* / *isn't* a window in the picture.

2 ★★ **Look at the picture and complete the questions and answers with the correct form of *there is/there are*.**

1 Is there________ any juice?
Yes________, there is________.
2 ________ any bananas?
________, there ________.
3 ________ any tomatoes?
________, there ________.
4 ________ any cheese?
________, there ________.
5 ________ any milk?
________, there ________.

Much/Many, A Lot Of

3 ★★ **Circle the correct options.**

My sister loves cooking, and she has [1]*a lot of* / *much* ideas for delicious meals. I like cooking, too, but I don't have [2]*many* / *much* time to help her. She often uses [3]*a lot of* / *much* fruit and vegetables. She loves healthy food. Tonight, she wants to make pasta for dinner, but there isn't [4]*many* / *much* pasta, and there aren't [5]*many* / *much* tomatoes in the fridge. The good thing is that there are [6]*a lot of* / *much* restaurants near home!

4 ★★ **Complete the questions in the quiz with *much* or *many*. Then circle the correct answers.**

HOW MUCH DO YOU KNOW?

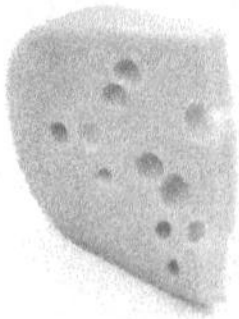

1 How ________ milk is there in 1kg of cheese?
a two liters b five liters

2 How ________ water is there in a banana?
a 74% b 90%

3 How ________ sugar is there in an average glass of orange juice?
a about 21 g b about 50 g

4 How ________ coffee beans are there in a 1-kg bag of coffee?
a about 1,500 b about 8,800

5 ★★★ **Look in your fridge and answer the questions.**

1 How much fruit is there?
____

2 How many vegetables are there?
____

WRITING
A Description

1 ☆ **Look at the menus and read the description. Which menu is from Eva's favorite place, a or b?**

____

My Favorite Place to Eat

by Eva García

1 My name's Eva [1]*and* / *but* I'm from Chile. My favorite place to eat is a small café called Buenas Migas. I go there every Friday with my best friend and our parents.

2 Buenas Migas is near my house. There isn't a lot of space inside the café [2]*and* / *or* it doesn't have many tables, [3]*or* / *but* there are some more tables outside. We sit outside when the weather's nice.

3 You can eat different sandwiches, and they're all delicious! They have egg, cheese, chicken, [4]*but* / *or* meat sandwiches and they're all healthy. My favorite is the egg sandwich.

4 To drink, you can have water, soda, [5]*but* / *or* juice. Their orange and carrot juice is always fresh. It's definitely my favorite drink!

a

b

2 ☆☆ **Circle the correct options in the description.**

3 ☆☆ **Circle the correct options.**

We use [1]*but* / *or* when there is a choice (usually between two things).

We use [2]*but* / *and* to contrast different information.

We use [3]*or* / *and* to add similar information.

4 ☆☆ **Read the description again. Match topics a–d with paragraphs 1–4.**

a food (including your favorite) [3]

b introduction: who you are, what the description is about [ ]

c drinks (including your favorite) [ ]

d the place: where it is and what it is like [ ]

PLAN

5 ☆☆ **Write a description of your favorite place to eat. Make notes about the place. Say where it is, when you go there, and what it is like. Decide what information to include in each paragraph. Use the information in Exercise 4 to help you.**

WRITE

6 ☆☆☆ **Write your description. Remember to include four paragraphs, *there is* / *there are*, countable and uncountable nouns, and expressions from the *Useful Language* box (see Student's Book, p53).**

CHECK

7 Do you ...

- introduce yourself and say where you are from and the name of your favorite place?
- say what your favorite type of food and drink is?
- use adjectives to describe food?

4 REVIEW

VOCABULARY

1 Write the food or drink words. Use the picture to help you.

1 They are a vegetable. They are long and orange. _ _ _ _ _ _ _

2 You can make cheese from this drink. _ _ _ _

3 It's usually brown and it's sweet. It's made from cacao. _ _ _ _ _ _ _ _ _

4 It's usually on top of pizza. _ _ _ _ _ _

5 They come from chickens. _ _ _ _

6 It's a yellow fruit. There are a lot in Ecuador. _ _ _ _ _ _

7 You make this drink with fruit or vegetables. _ _ _ _ _

8 It's a drink, but we also use it to take a shower. _ _ _ _ _

2 Match the opposites.

1 healthy ☐ a disgusting
2 delicious ☐ b sweet
3 cold ☐ c unhealthy
4 salty ☐ d hot

GRAMMAR IN ACTION

3 Circle the correct option: *C* (countable) or *U* (uncountable).

1 apple *C / U*
2 cheese *C / U*
3 water *C / U*
4 sandwich *C / U*
5 bread *C / U*
6 milk *C / U*
7 potato *C / U*
8 chocolate *C / U*
9 banana *C / U*
10 bean *C / U*

4 Complete the text with *a*, *some*, or *any*.

It's my mom's birthday today, and my dad and I want to make her a nice meal. We don't have [1] __________ chicken, but we have [2] __________ meat to cook with [3] __________ rice. There's [4] __________ bottle of water in the fridge and we have [5] __________ fruit juice, too. There are [6] __________ carrots and [7] __________ tomatoes as well. We have [8] __________ book for my mom. She loves reading.

5 Complete the conversation with the words and phrases in the box.

Are there any	How many	Is there	
much	some	there are	There aren't

NATHAN Let's make dinner.

ANDREA OK. We can cook some chicken with vegetables. [1] __________ vegetables?

NATHAN Yes, [2] __________. We have three carrots and some tomatoes.

ANDREA [3] __________ tomatoes are there? I need three.

NATHAN [4] __________ three – only two.

ANDREA OK. [5] __________ any cheese? We can have the tomatoes with some cheese.

NATHAN Yes, there's [6] __________ cheese!

ANDREA Great. And how [7] __________ chicken is there?

NATHAN A lot! We can eat chicken for dinner, breakfast, and lunch!

CUMULATIVE GRAMMAR

6 Complete the conversation with the missing words. Circle the correct options.

VICTOR Mom, what [1] __________ for dinner?

MOM There's [2] __________ soup and fish. Do you want that?

VICTOR Yes, I'm hungry! And [3] __________ can I have to drink?

MOM [4] __________ some soda.

VICTOR Do we have any juice? I don't like [5] __________ soda.

MOM Take a look in the fridge. I think there [6] __________ two bottles of juice there.

VICTOR Yes! And it's orange juice – delicious! Do you want some juice, too?

MOM No, thanks. I [7] __________ like it very much. I prefer water. [8] __________ any apples for after your dinner?

VICTOR No, there [9] __________ any, but there are some bananas. I [10] __________ eat those.

MOM You're hungry! There's [11] __________ food, and you can eat all of it!

VICTOR OK, Mom. Yes, I'm really hungry!

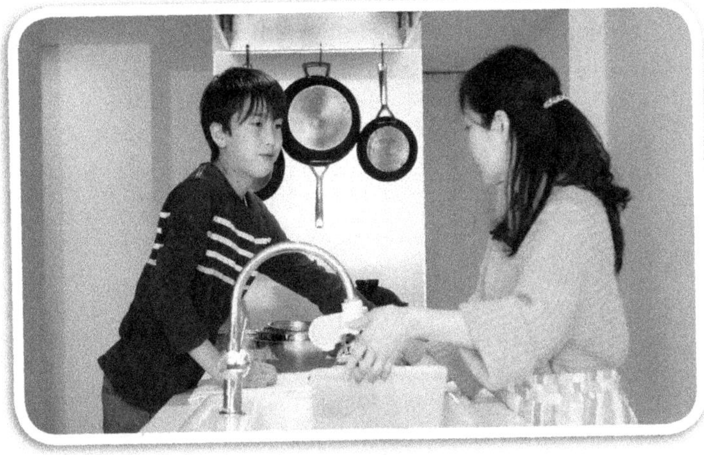

1 a there is b is there c are there
2 a some b a c an
3 a where b what c when
4 a There are b There is c There has
5 a drink b drinking c drinks
6 a are b have c is
7 a do b don't c 'm not
8 a Are there b Is there c Are they
9 a aren't b isn't c haven't
10 a am b do c can
11 a much b a lot of c many

5 What's your style?

VOCABULARY

Clothes

1 ☆ Look at the photos and circle the correct words.

1 *boots* / *sneakers*
2 *hoodie* / *T-shirt*
3 *jeans* / *sweatpants*
4 *boots* / *flip-flops*
5 *shorts* / *skirt*
6 *T-shirt* / *jacket*

2 ☆ Look at the picture. Complete the text with the words in the box.

boots	cap	jacket	shirt
shorts	sneakers	sweatpants	~~T-shirt~~

Laura's favorite outfit is a [1] T-shirt, [2] ______, [3] ______, and a [4] ______. Alex's favorite outfit is a [5] ______ and a [6] ______, [7] ______, and [8] ______.

3 ☆☆☆ What can you wear? Write at least three clothes items for each situation.

1 Your friends ask you to go to the mountains with them in December.
I can wear ______
2 It's July and you have a picnic with your parents.
______
3 It's Saturday afternoon and you want to visit your grandma.
______

Explore It!

Guess the correct answer.

A *kurta* is a long shirt without a collar. Men and women from *South America* / *South Asia* / *Europe* wear kurtas.

Find another interesting fact about clothes in your country. Write a question and send it to a classmate in an email, or ask them in the next class.

READING

An Online Diary

1 Read Marina's online diary. Who doesn't like purple?

____

Marina'sFashionFriends.com

Sunday, 10:30 a.m.

It's Sunday morning and I'm writing this post from the park. I'm here with my family. I can see a group of girls. They're talking and having some snacks. One girl looks great! I want her clothes! She's wearing purple jeans, an orange T-shirt, a black cap, and some fabulous purple sneakers.  I think those sneakers are in a store around the corner! Hmm … do I have got the money to buy them?

2:00 p.m. (and back online!)

I'm at home and guess what? I have those beautiful sneakers!

6:00 p.m.

Comments

Ethan: Hi, Marina! I always read your diary, and I usually like your ideas. But sorry … I don't like purple. I think it's a horrible color! It's a nice day today and I'm at a park, too. I'm wearing my new sweatpants, and a T-shirt, but it's hot now, and I'm not wearing my cap. What are you wearing?

Ada: Where can I buy those sneakers? I want some, too. Ethan, purple is THE color! I have six purple T-shirts and a pair of purple shorts! I'm wearing my favorite purple T-shirt today!

8:00 p.m.

Ada, they're selling them in World of Sneakers. I'm wearing them now!
Now I need some jeans. 
Sorry, Ethan, purple is THE color!

New post tomorrow!

2 **Read the diary again and <u>underline</u> these words. Check their meaning in a dictionary and then complete the sentences.**

beautiful	corner	~~fabulous~~	guess what	pair

1 I love my green boots. They're <u>fabulous</u>!
2 ______________ ? We're in the same class!
3 The store isn't far away. It's around the ______________ .
4 Sara's new skirt is ______________ . I want one!
5 You need to get a new ______________ of shoes.

3 **Read the diary again. Circle the correct answers.**

1 It's Sunday and Marina *is* / (*isn't*) at home.
2 She likes *one girl's* / *some girls'* sneakers.
3 Ethan *usually likes* / *doesn't usually like* Marina's posts.
4 Marina and *Ethan* / *Ada* want to buy the sneakers.
5 Ada *has some* / *doesn't have any* purple clothes.
6 Marina tells *Ethan* / *Ada* the name of a sneakers store.

4 **Answer the questions with your own ideas.**

1 Do you think fashion is important? Why / Why not?

____

____

2 Where do you get your ideas about what to wear? For example, from online diaries, friends, magazines, TV, movies, stores?

____

____

GRAMMAR IN ACTION

Present Continuous

1 **Write the words in the correct order to make sentences.**

1 on TV / I'm / fashion show / a / watching

I'm watching a fashion show on TV.

2 her / She / isn't / doing / homework

____

3 the park / sitting / Marina / is / in

____

4 a / Ethan / isn't / cap / wearing

____

5 playing / We're / basketball

____

6 same / skirt / the / buying / They're

____

2 **Complete the message with the correct form of the verb *to be*.**

60%

< Back

Hi Dad! I [1] *'m* sitting on the school bus and it [2] ________ (not) moving! The bus driver [3] ________ talking on the phone, and he [4] ________ (not) looking very happy. Oh, and it [5] ________ raining! Can you come? Juan [6] ________ playing hockey, and Mom [7] ________ (not) answering the phone.
Thanks, Dad!

3 **What are they doing? Look at pictures 1–4 and write sentences using the words in boxes a and b.**

a: dance ~~read~~ ride write

b: a bike ~~a magazine~~ on the board to music

1 *He's reading a magazine.*

2 ____________________

3 ____________________

4 ____________________

4 **Match questions 1–6 with answers a–f.**

1 Are you listening to me? [b]
2 Is Anton wearing his new sneakers? [ ]
3 Is Claudia studying? [ ]
4 What are they eating? [ ]
5 Which movie is Pedro watching? [ ]
6 Where are you having your lunch? [ ]

a *Wonder Woman*.
b ~~Yes, I am~~!
c In the cafeteria.
d No, she isn't.
e Cold pizza. Yuck!
f Yes, he is.

5 **Answer the questions.**

1 What are you wearing today?

____

2 What is your best friend doing now?

____

6 **Find out what two people in your family are doing now. Write sentences in the present continuous.**

My sister's watching TV.

____

____

____

1

3

2

4

VOCABULARY AND LISTENING

Accessories

1 ☆ Complete the accessory words in the spidergram.

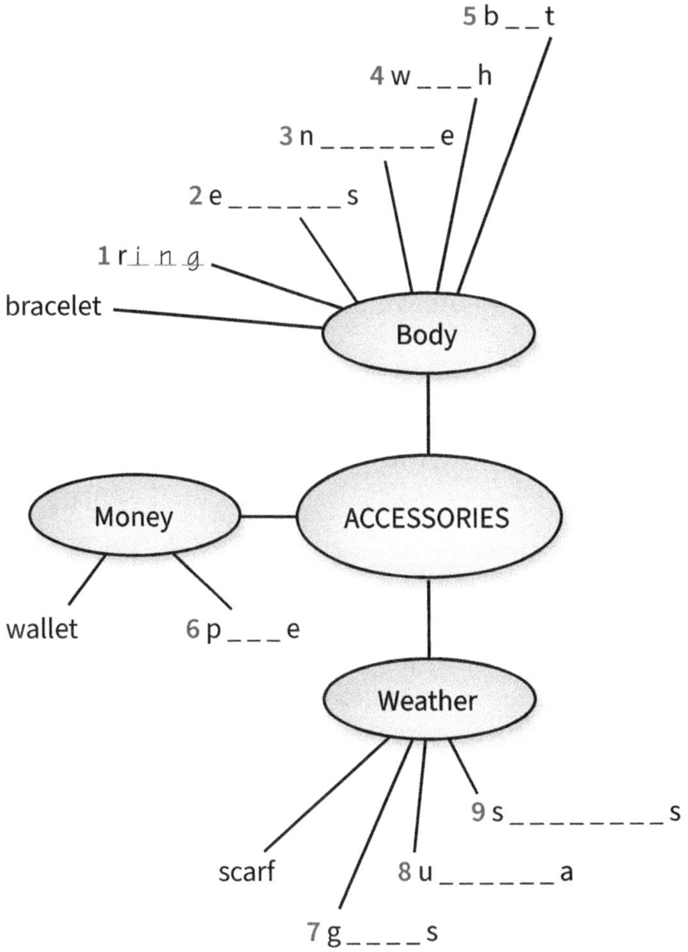

2 ☆☆ Complete the sentences with words from Exercise 1.

1 Those new jeans look big. You need a *belt*.

2 José always wears ______________ when it's sunny.

3 Madison carries her wallet and phone in her ______________.

4 I don't wear a ______________ because there's a clock in the classroom.

5 It's raining, and I don't have my ______________!

6 In cold weather, my grandma always wears ______________ and a ______________.

7 My dad has a big ______________, but he never has any money in it!

An Interview

5.01 3 ☆ Listen to the interview. Mark (✓) the two things that Alba paints.

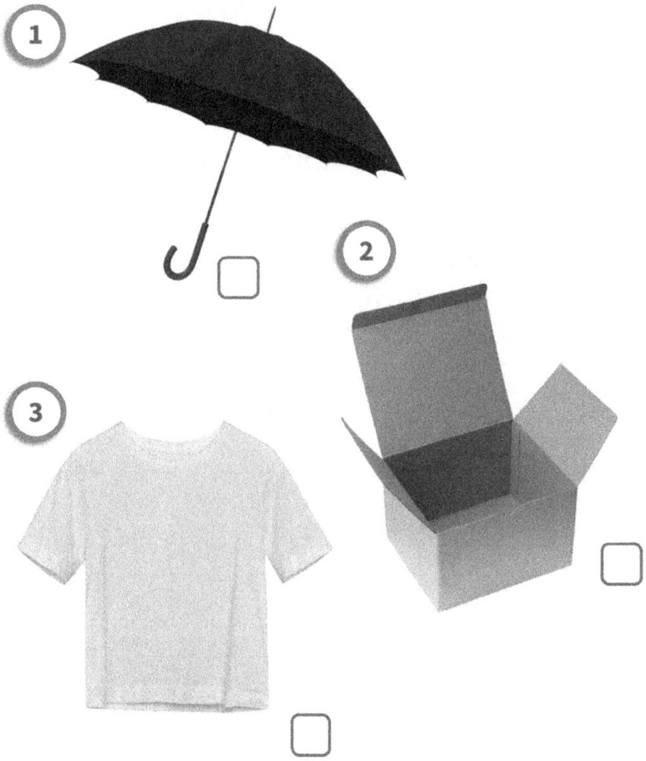

5.01 4 ☆☆☆ Listen again. Answer the questions.

1 Who is Alba painting this week?
Her baby brother.

2 Where does she get her ideas from?
____

3 What does she put in the mini boxes?
____

4 What is inside the box for her friend?
____

5 What does the interviewer want?
____

5 ☆ Alba is making you a box (big or small). Write two things you want to put in it. Use the ideas below or your own ideas.

a bracelet	a ring	a wallet	a watch	gloves

I'd like ______________ and ______________.

GRAMMAR IN ACTION

Simple Present and Present Continuous

1 ★ Circle the correct options.

2 We use the *simple present* / *present continuous* to talk about things happening now.

3 We use the *simple present* / *present continuous* to talk about facts, habits, and routines.

2 ★ Complete the chart with the words and phrases in the box.

at the moment every Monday never ~~on Fridays~~ right now sometimes this week this morning today usually

Facts, Habits, and Routines	Things Happening Now
on Fridays	______
______	______
______	______
______	______
______	______

3 ★★ Write sentences with the simple present or present continuous.

1 Some people / wear / sports clothes / on the weekend

Some people wear sports clothes on the weekend.

2 I / look for / some jeans / right now

______

3 They / make / the costumes for the show / now

______

4 Naomi / usually / buy / red clothes

______

5 We / never / go shopping / on Saturdays

______

6 A lot of people / wear / hats / at the moment

______

4 ★★ Complete the conversation with the simple present or present continuous form of the verbs in parentheses.

DANA What [1] are you doing (do), Paula?

PAULA I [2] ______ (look) at my clothes. Some of them are very small now. I [3] ______ (often / need) new clothes in the summer.

DANA Oh! Can I have this skirt?

PAULA Well, I [4] ______ (always / give) my small clothes to my little sister, but she [5] ______ (not wear) skirts, so it's yours!

DANA Thanks! Where [6] ______ (you / usually / buy) your clothes?

PAULA At a store near home. My mom [7] ______ (shop) there right now.

DANA [8] ______ (they / sell) accessories, too? I [9] ______ (look for) a bracelet at the moment.

PAULA Yes, they do! They [10] ______ (sell) lovely bracelets. We can go shopping there together next time!

5 ★★★ Answer the questions.

1 What do you do with your old clothes and accessories?

______

2 What clothes are you wearing a lot at the moment?

______

3 What do you usually wear in the evening during the week?

______

WRITING

A Description of a Photo

1 ☆ **Read the description and look at the photo. Write the names of the people (a–e).**

a Damir
b ______
c ______
d ______
e ______

A Photo of a Day Out
By Alyssa

1 This is a photo of my friends and me. We're on a school trip to a national park. It's cold but sunny.

2 The boy on the left is Damir. He [1]*looks* / *'s looking* down. He often [2]*looks* / *is looking* down because he hates photos! He [3]*wears* / *'s wearing* a black and gray hoodie. Next to Damir is Peter. He's in a pink shirt and a gray sweater. The boys [4]*don't wear* / *aren't wearing* jackets in the photo. Then that's me in the middle, with a jacket and a checked shirt. Carmen's next to me. She [5]*wears* / *'s wearing* her favorite denim jacket and a big scarf. Gina's on the right. She has a gray T-shirt, a green jacket, and a scarf. Gina's the only one in a hat.

3 This is one of my favorite photos. We [6]*laugh* / *'re laughing* because it's a fun day. I like this photo because there are trees in the back and we all look happy. We always [7]*have* / *are having* a great time!

2 ☆☆ **Circle the correct form of the verbs (1–7) in the description.**

3 ☆☆ **Read the description again. Complete the sentences with the words in the box.**

Alyssa	boys	girls	Peter	~~trees~~

1 The trees are in the back.
2 ______ is in the middle. Carmen and ______ are next to her.
3 The ______ are on the left.
4 The ______ are on the right.

4 ☆☆ **Match topics a–c with paragraphs 1–3.**

a why it is a favorite photo ☐
b people in the photo, where they are, and what they're wearing ☐
c who is in the photo and where the photo is ☐

PLAN

5 ☆☆ **Write your own description of a photo of a day out. Choose your photo and make notes. Decide what information to include in each paragraph. Use the information in Exercise 4 to help you.**

WRITE

6 ☆☆☆ **Write your description. Remember to include the information in the correct order, the simple present and present continuous, and expressions from the *Useful Language* box (see Student's Book, p65).**

CHECK

7 Do you …

- describe the people in the photo, including the clothes and accessories they are wearing?
- describe the people's positions in the photo?
- say why you like the photo?

5 REVIEW

VOCABULARY

1 **Circle the word that doesn't fit.**

1 sweatpants / T-shirt / jeans
2 sneakers / shorts / boots
3 shorts / boots / skirt
4 jacket / hoodie / cap
5 shirt / skirt / shorts
6 flip-flops / boots / sneakers

2 **Complete the crossword. Use the pictures.**

ACROSS →

3

6
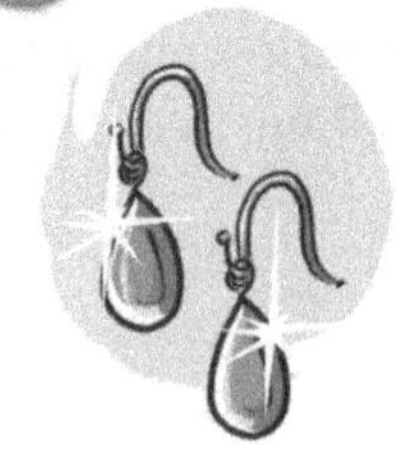

8

9
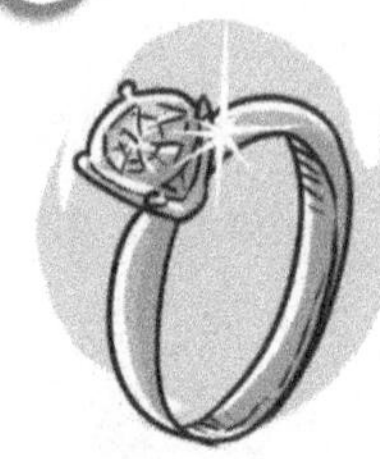

10
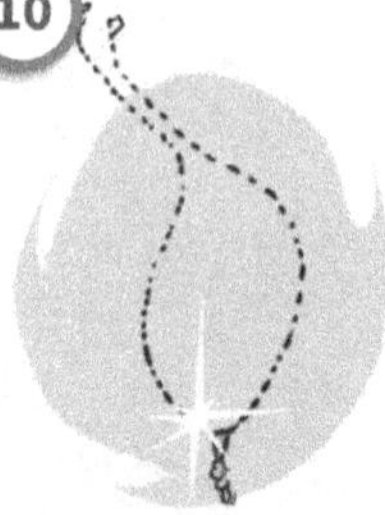

11

DOWN ↓

1

2
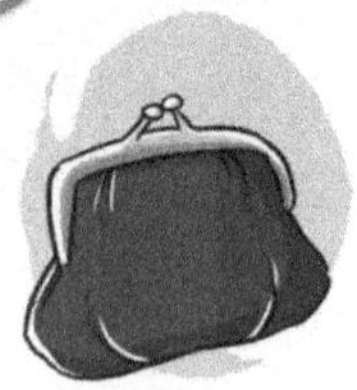

4

5

7

8

GRAMMAR IN ACTION

3 **Complete the sentences with the present continuous form of the verbs in the box.**

do	look	make	not rain	not wear	watch

1 **A:** What ________________ you ________________ now?
B: I'm doing my homework.
2 At the moment, I ________________ for a new jacket with my dad.
3 They ________________ a TV show about the history of fashion.
4 We ________________ our school clothes today – it's Sunday.
5 My grandma ________________ me a new dress for my birthday.
6 You don't need an umbrella. It ________________.

4 Circle the correct options.

MAYA	What [1]*do you usually do / are you usually doing* on the weekend?
ISAAC	We [2]*sometimes visit / are sometimes visiting* my grandparents, but they [3]*travel / 're traveling* around Europe at the moment.

LILY	[4]*Is Jimi having / Does Jimi have* lunch at home this month?
TOM	Yes. He usually [5]*has / is having* lunch at school, but this month he [6]*goes / 's going* home early.

HUGO	[7]*Does Dad do / Is Dad doing* the shopping now?
CALEB	No, it's Sunday. The stores [8]*close / are closing* early on Sundays.

CUMULATIVE GRAMMAR

5 Complete the conversation with the missing words. Circle the correct options.

ADAM	Hi, Mom. [1]__________ are you?
MOM	Hi, Adam! I'm [2]__________ the shopping with Dad.
ADAM	Oh, OK! Listen, [3]__________ for a bike ride this afternoon with Tom and his brother?
MOM	Sure! We don't have [4]__________ plans.
ADAM	Great! But [5]__________ a problem. I can't [6]__________ my sneakers, or my hoodie. Where are they?
MOM	I [7]__________ know. They're your things.
ADAM	Oh! The sneakers are under my bed, but I can't see my hoodie. Can you buy [8]__________ a new one, please?
MOM	A new one? I don't have [9]__________ time now, and you have a hoodie! You need to look for [10]__________.
ADAM	Ugh! I hate [11]__________ things.
MOM	I know, but how often [12]__________ things when you look for them?
ADAM	Hmm, I guess so. OK, talk to you later.

1	a When	b Where	c What
2	a does	b do	c doing
3	a can I go	b I can go	c do I go
4	a any	b some	c a
5	a there are	b there's	c it's
6	a find	b to find	c finding
7	a not	b 'm not	c don't
8	a me	b it	c my
9	a many	b any	c a lot
10	a it	b they	c them
11	a look for	b looking for	c looks for
12	a are you finding	b do you find	c you find

6 How can we be athletic?

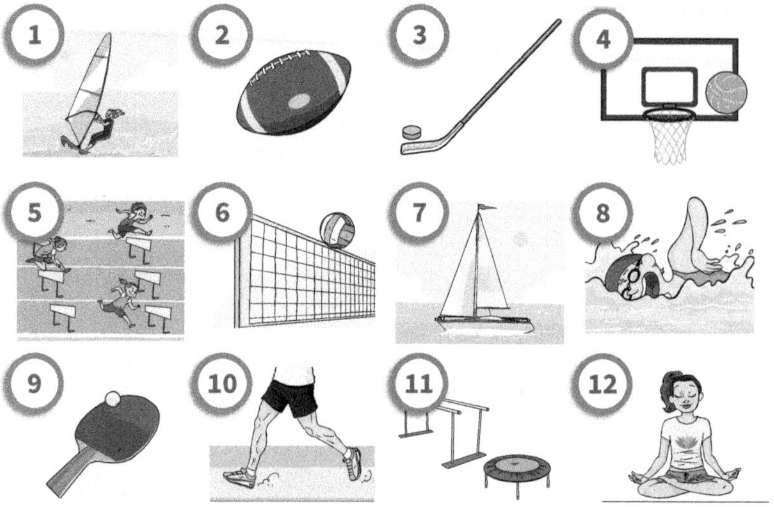

VOCABULARY

Sports

1 ☆ **Complete the word puzzle. Use the pictures (1–12). What is the mystery word in gray?**

2 ☆☆ **Complete the rules with *play*, *do*, or *go*.**

We usually use [1]________ with sports that end in *-ing*.

We usually use [2]________ with sports with balls and other objects.

We usually use [3]________ with other sports.

3 ☆☆ **Circle the correct options.**

I like playing sports. At school, we do [1]*running* / *track and field* and I like that. Sometimes on the weekend I go [2]*swimming* / *yoga* with my brother. He does [3]*gymnastics* / *football* at an after-school gym and goes [4]*running* / *table tennis* twice a week. I don't really like team sports, but in the summer, I sometimes play [5]*sailing* / *volleyball* with my friends on the beach. And I love going [6]*yoga* / *rock climbing* with my dad in the mountains.

4 ☆☆☆ **Answer the questions.**

1 What are your favorite sports?

____

2 Do you play sports at school? Which sports?

____

Explore It!

Guess the correct answer.

Which sport comes from Canada?

a hockey b table tennis c football

Find another interesting fact about sports in your country. Write a question and send it to a classmate in an email, or ask them in the next class.

READING
Online FAQs

1 ☆ **Read the article. What sport is it about? Mark (✓) the correct photo (1–3).**

1
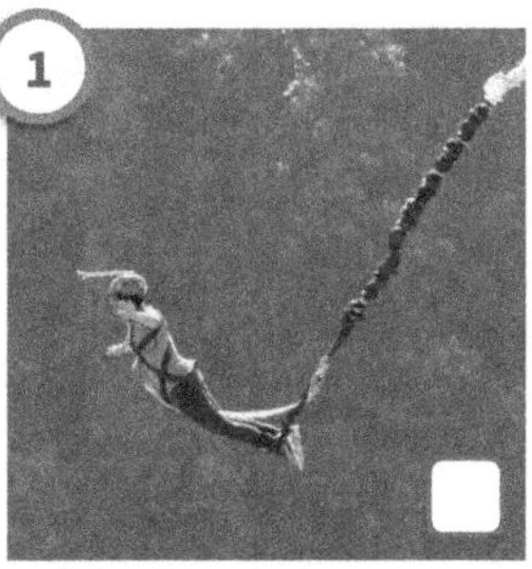

2

3
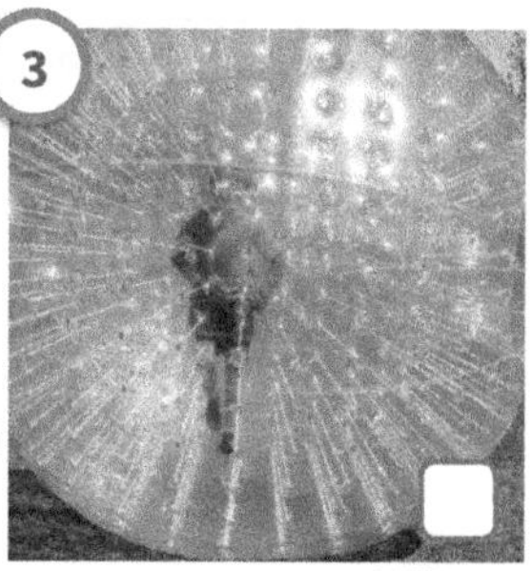

FUN IN THE SUN!

Are you looking for a new sport? Do you want to try something more exciting? In New Zealand, we have the answer – try zorbing! It's new and it's different!

FAQs

Q1: What is Zorbing?

Zorbing is a fun outdoor sport. It's more popular here in New Zealand than in other countries.

Q2: ____________________

You need a large plastic ball. This is called a zorb. You get inside the ball and run or walk. When you move, the ball moves, too! You know where you're going and how you're moving because you can see through the ball. A lot of people love going down a hill in their zorb. It's exciting!

Q3: ____________________

No, it's an individual sport. You get inside the zorb on your own, but it's really fun to go with family or friends because you can have races – sometimes children are faster than their parents!

Q4: ____________________

Yes, it is, but always do it in a zorbing center and follow the rules. Have fun, but be careful – don't get hurt!

Q5: ____________________

Yes. To go zorbing, you usually need to be six years old or older.

Q6: ____________________

There are zorbing centers in many places on the South Island. Click here for a list of centers.

Q7: ____________________

Yes, it's more expensive than other traditional sports, but it's a great activity for special days. So, are you ready for zorbing? What are you waiting for!

2 ☆☆ **Read the article again. Complete it with the missing questions.**

a Is there an age limit?
b Is it a team sport?
c What do you do?
d ~~What is zorbing~~?
e Where can I do it?
f Is it expensive?
g Is it safe?

3 ☆☆ **Read the article again and underline these words. Then check their meaning in a dictionary and complete the sentences.**

| get hurt | hill | race | ~~safe~~ | try |

1 Be careful! Going out alone at night isn't safe.
2 The Spartathlon is a __________ in Greece. People run 246 kilometers!
3 I live at the top of a __________. Walking down to school is easy!
4 I love tennis, but this year I want to __________ a new sport.
5 Careful there! You can fall and __________!

4 ☆☆☆ **Answer the questions.**

1 Do you want to try zorbing? Why / Why not?

____

2 What fun outdoor sports are popular in your country?

____

GRAMMAR IN ACTION

Comparatives

1 ☆ **Write the comparative forms.**

1 small smaller
2 big ______
3 good ______
4 happy ______
5 interesting ______
6 bad ______

2 ☆ **Complete the rules with the adjectives from Exercise 1.**

1 For one-syllable adjectives, add *-er*: smaller.
2 For two-syllable adjectives ending in *-y*, remove the *-y* and add *-ier*: ______.
3 For long adjectives, add *more* before the adjective: ______.
4 For one-syllable adjectives ending in a vowel and a consonant, double the consonant and add *-er*: ______.
5 For irregular adjectives, use a different word: ______ and ______.

3 ☆☆ **<u>Underline</u> and correct one mistake in each sentence.**

1 Windsurfing is more expensive <u>that</u> running. than
2 Basketball is more fast than football. ______
3 Runners are usually thiner than swimmers. ______
4 Which sport is noisyer, volleyball, or yoga? ______
5 She's badder at gymastics than at hockey. ______
6 Playing sports is more better than watching it. ______

4 ☆☆ **Complete the sentences with the comparative form of the adjectives in parentheses.**

1 A hockey match is longer than a basketball game. (long)
2 I think rock climbing is ______ than yoga. (exciting)
3 Lola's ______ at tennis than her dad. (good)
4 Our school hockey team is ______ than the football team. (bad)
5 We think soccer is a ______ game than football. (difficult)
6 Playing sports is ______ than watching TV. (healthy)

5 ☆☆ **Complete the questions with a comparative adjective. Then check the answers at the bottom of the page.**

DANIEL Let's do this quiz! First question: Which ball is [1] faster, a table tennis or a tennis ball?
ANIYAH A table tennis ball?
DANIEL Next question: Which is [2] ______, a basketball game or a hockey match?
ANIYAH I don't know. Hockey?
DANIEL Number three: Which country is [3] ______ at table tennis, China or South Korea?
ANIYAH South Korea, I think.
DANIEL And the last question: Which sport is [4] ______ in schools here in New Zealand, hockey or track and field?
ANIYAH Oh, no! I don't know. Track and field maybe. What are the answers?

6 ☆☆☆ **Write three sentences comparing sports. Look at Exercise 4 to help you.**

I think soccer is more entertaining than football.
______
______
______

Answers

1 table tennis ball: 116 km/h; tennis ball: 263 km/h
2 hockey match: 60 minutes; basketball game: 48 minutes
3 China (1); South Korea (2)
4 number of people playing in schools in New Zealand: hockey: 13,967, track and field: 12,713

VOCABULARY AND LISTENING

Sports Verbs

1 ☆ Match photos 1–6 with six of the sports verbs a–l.

a ~~bounce~~	b catch	c climb	d dive	e hit	f jump
g kick	h lift	i pass	j run	k score	l throw

1

2

3

4

5

6

2 ☆☆ (Circle) the correct verbs.

I don't understand rugby! OK, the players [1](pass) / *score* the ball to each other. Then they [2]*catch / run* up the field and put the ball over a line to [3]*score / hit* points. They also [4]*kick / jump* the ball over a big goalpost. But sometimes the teams make a circle and push each other. Then one player [5]*scores / throws* the ball into the circle and another player from the same team gets it. And sometimes some players [6]*lift / jump* on top of other players!

3 ☆☆☆ Write two sentences describing what players can and can't do in a sport. Use the sports verbs from Exercise 1.

In soccer, the players can kick the ball, but they can't score goals with their hands.

____

____

____

A Conversation

4 ☆ Look at the photo and listen to a conversation about goalball, a sport for people who are visually impaired. (Circle) the correct answers. (6.01)

1 Goalball players use a special ball with *lights / sound*.

2 Goalball is *a team / an individual* sport.

5 ☆☆☆ Listen again. Complete the sentences with one word. (6.01)

1 The goalball ball is like a basketball, but heavier.

2 A goalball team has __________ players on it.

3 Players try to __________ the ball to score a goal.

4 They use their __________ to stop the ball.

5 Some players throw the ball __________ kilometers per hour.

6 Jon plays goalball on a __________ court.

7 The boy wants to watch Jon's match on __________.

6 ☆☆☆ Watch part of a Paralympics goalball match on the Internet. Then write three things you like about it.

I like how the players throw the ball.

____

____

____

____

GRAMMAR IN ACTION

Superlatives

1 ☆ **Complete the chart with the superlative form of the adjectives in the box.**

bad ~~entertaining~~ fit healthy old

The most + adjective	*The* + double the final consonant + *-est*	*The* + change *y* to *i* + *-est*	*The* + adjective + *-est*	*The* + irregular form
the most popular	2 ______	the easiest	4 ______	the best
1 the most entertaining	the biggest	3 ______	the fastest	5 ______

2 ☆☆ **Complete the text with the superlative form of the adjectives in parentheses.**

My cousin Nick is the 1 most popular (popular) person in my family. He's the 2 ______ (tall) of my cousins and also the 3 ______ (fit) – on the weekend, he does yoga and plays hockey! Everybody loves Nick.

He's the 4 ______ (happy) person I know! I'm the 5 ______ (young) person in my family and the 6 ______ (bad) at sports! But that's OK because we're all different. I love reading and writing stories. Nick says I write the 7 ______ (interesting) stories in the world.

3 ☆☆ **Write the questions in the quiz using the superlative form of the adjectives. Then circle the correct answers. Check your answers at the bottom of the quiz!**

SPORTS QUESTION TIME!

1 Which is / popular / sport in Brazil?
Which is the most popular sport in Brazil?
a basketball **(b)** soccer

2 Which is one of the / old / ball sports?
______
a Ulama from Mexico
b Alama from Ecuador

3 Which is one of the / new / sports?
______
a table tennis
b 360Ball

4 Which is one of the / difficult / sports for many people?
______
a rock climbing **b** running

5 Which is one of the / expensive / sports in the world?
______
a tennis **b** swimming

ANSWERS
1 b 2 a 3 b 4 a 5 a

4 ☆☆☆ **Complete the questions with the superlative form of the adjectives. Then answer them for you.**

1 Who is the youngest (young) person in your family?
______

2 Which is ______ (popular) sport at your school?
______

3 Which is ______ (difficult) school subject?
______

4 Which is ______ (entertaining) movie you know?
______

WRITING

A Profile of an Athlete

1 ★ **Look at the photos and read the profile. Then complete the sentence.**

For Ivan, Natalia Partyka is an ______________ athlete because she plays table tennis with ______________.

A Popular Athlete from My Country

By Ivan Nowak

1 I'm from Poland, and I think one of the [1]*more / most* popular athletes from my country is Natalia Partyka. She's a table tennis player. She's 1.73 m tall and weighs 64 kg. She only has one hand and part of her right arm.

2 Natalia trains for about six hours a day. She often plays with her [2]*older / more older* sister, Sandra. Sometimes she practices bouncing the ball on the top part of her arm to begin the game. In her free time, Natalia loves reading the letters from her fans. She also likes going to the beach with her friends.

3 I think Natalia is the [3]*more / most* amazing athlete from my country because she plays with one hand. She's also an excellent athlete – she's part of the Paralympic team and the Olympic Games team, too. She has more gold medals than any other table tennis player in Poland, and she's one of the [4]*most / more* successful players in the world, too.

2 ★★ **Circle the correct options (1–4) in the profile.**

3 ★★ **Read the profile again. Underline two sentences with *also* and two sentences with *too*. Then complete the rules with *also* or *too*.**

We use *too* and *also* to give extra information. We use [1]__________ at the end of a sentence. We use [2]__________ after the verb *to be* and before other verbs.

4 ★★ **Read the profile again. Match topics a–c with paragraphs 1–3.**

a training and other interests ☐
b achievements ☐
c basic information and description ☐

PLAN

5 ★★ **Write a profile of a popular athlete from your country. Make notes about the athlete. Decide what information to include in each paragraph. Use the information in Exercise 4 to help you.**

WRITE

6 ★★★ **Write your profile. Remember to include three paragraphs, comparatives and superlatives, and expressions from the *Useful Language* box (see Student's Book, p77).**

CHECK

7 **Do you ...**

- give basic information and a description of your athlete?
- describe their sport using sports verbs?
- talk about their achievements and why you like them?

6 REVIEW

VOCABULARY

1 Complete the chart with the sports in the box.

football running sailing
swimming tennis track and field
volleyball windsurfing yoga

Water Sports	Ball Sports	Other Sports

2 Find 12 sports verbs in the word search.

B	D	I	B	T	D	I	V	E	H
U	I	C	S	D	Q	H	G	R	I
V	0	L	I	F	T	A	H	B	T
Y	K	I	C	K	R	Z	O	S	P
E	C	M	W	Q	M	N	S	C	A
N	P	B	O	U	N	C	E	O	L
L	Y	K	J	C	J	A	T	R	U
T	H	R	O	W	V	T	G	E	R
H	J	U	M	P	W	C	E	F	U
F	P	A	S	S	K	H	X	G	N

3 Complete the sentences with the correct form of the verbs from Exercise 2.

1 A basketball player b__________ the ball on the court.
2 My brother loves j__________ on the bed!
3 Mount Everest, the highest mountain in the world, is very difficult to c__________.
4 We never s__________ many goals in soccer.
5 Tennis players can't h__________ the ball with their hands. They use a racket.
6 In gymnastics, we sometimes l__________ heavy boxes to make our arms strong.

GRAMMAR IN ACTION

4 Write sentences using the comparative form of the adjectives in parentheses.

1 zorbing / running (exciting)
____
2 water / soda (healthy)
____
3 sweatpants / jeans (comfortable)
____
4 a table tennis ball / a tennis ball (small)
____
5 jumping / rock climbing (easy)
____

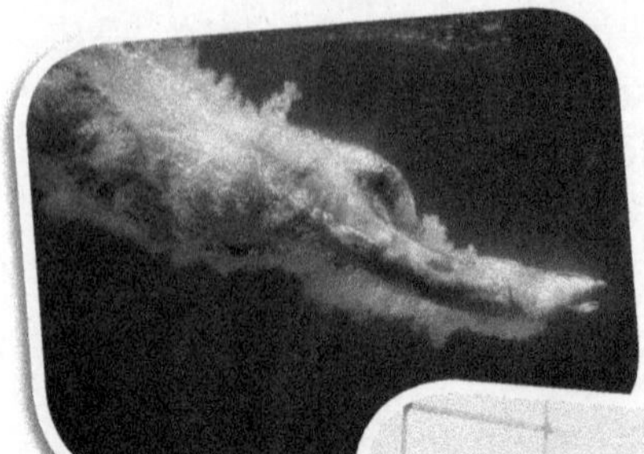

5 Complete the text with the superlative form of the adjectives in parentheses.

I think tennis is the [1] ______________ (boring) sport, but my dad loves it! At the moment, he's in London at the All England Club. This club is the [2] ______________ (old) in the world. Every year, there are different tennis tournaments there. The [3] ______________ (popular) one is called Wimbledon. My dad says all the [4] ______________ (good) players want to win there. People watching tennis at Wimbledon don't usually speak to each other a lot. The [5] ______________ (bad) thing you can do at Wimbledon is talk! The players don't like noise. I think the [6] ______________ (easy) thing is to watch Wimbledon on TV, but not for me – I prefer a good movie!

CUMULATIVE GRAMMAR

6 Complete the conversation with the missing words. Circle the correct options.

ESMA Which sports [1] ______________ you like, Rafael?

RAFAEL I like [2] ______________ track and field and playing baseball.

ESMA I think baseball is the [3] ______________ sport in the world.

RAFAEL Me, too! Today, I [4] ______________ baseball practice and then yoga.

ESMA Yoga! I think it's [5] ______________ than track and field!

RAFAEL Then try it with me! I can teach you the [6] ______________ exercises.

ESMA Sounds great, but I'm the [7] ______________ student in the world!

RAFAEL Ah! But I'm a [8] ______________ teacher!

ESMA OK! I [9] ______________ try.

RAFAEL [10] ______________ your sweatpants in your bag?

ESMA No, but I can [11] ______________ home and get them now.

RAFAEL Perfect. Run home and bring [12] ______________ sweatpants!

	a	b	c
1	does	are	do
2	does	do	doing
3	best	better	good
4	has	have	having
5	most interesting	more interesting	interesting
6	more easy	most easy	easiest
7	bad	worse	worst
8	good	the better	best
9	can	have	do
10	Do you have	Do have	You have
11	go to	go	come
12	yours	you	your

7 Why are animals important?

VOCABULARY

Animals

1 ☆ **Find 13 more words for animals in the word search.**

C	R	O	C	O	D	I	L	E	D	E	Y
H	I	P	P	O	B	D	O	N	K	E	Y
J	L	S	I	S	W	A	Y	U	K	A	G
P	H	W	B	C	N	G	D	N	T	G	I
A	M	H	E	K	M	A	N	I	J	L	R
R	Q	O	A	V	I	D	K	T	H	E	A
R	K	R	R	P	L	U	Z	E	B	C	F
O	R	S	O	E	N	C	D	W	V	E	F
T	X	E	G	T	W	K	M	O	U	S	E
Z	F	W	H	A	L	E	G	K	S	B	A
A	N	F	M	P	B	M	O	N	K	E	Y
L	I	O	N	V	T	C	N	U	I	J	X

2 ☆ **Circle the animal in each category which is not correct. Then add a different animal to each category in the list.**

1 Birds	2 Mammals	3 Reptiles
duck	eagle	snake
hippo	giraffe	bear
parrot	lion	crocodile
______	______	______

3 ☆☆ **Read the descriptions and write the names of the animals from Exercise 1.**

1 This animal is a mammal. It usually lives in forests and cold places. It's very big and has a lot of hair. *bear*

2 This animal lives in water in hot countries. It's a reptile with a big mouth and a lot of big teeth. ______

3 This is a bird. It eats plants and it can swim and fly. It usually lives near water. ______

4 This animal likes cheese, but it doesn't like cats! It's usually gray and has a lot of babies. ______

5 This animal eats meat. It doesn't have any legs. Some of them can kill other animals and sometimes people, too. ______

6 This is a very large sea mammal. It has a hole on the top of its head. ______

4 ☆☆ **Choose another animal from Exercise 1 and write a definition.**

This animal is ______

______

______

______

Explore It!

Guess the correct answer.

Which bird sometimes sleeps with an eye open?

a duck b parrot c eagle

Find another interesting fact about birds. Write a question and send it to a classmate in an email, or ask them it in the next class.

READING

Fact Files

1 ☆ **Read the fact file below and circle the correct answers.**

1 Polar bears weigh …
  a about 360 kg.   b about 560 kg.
2 Polar bears live in …
  a the Arctic.   b the Antarctic.
3 Polar bears eat … of seal in a week.
  a about 35 kg   b about 55 kg

POLAR BEAR

Weight: about 360 kg
Habitat: the Arctic
Food: seals
Fact: Polar bears can smell a seal 32 km away! They can eat 55 kg of seal in a week.

2 ☆ **Read the article. What's special about the town of Churchill?** ____________

3 ☆☆ **Read the article again and underline these words. Then check their meaning in a dictionary and complete the sentences.**

attack	escape	hunt	~~ice~~	male	prison

1 In winter, there is ___ice___ on the river.
2 A female animal is a girl and a ____________ is a boy.
3 People can go to ____________ for killing an elephant.
4 Hungry lions are dangerous, and they sometimes ____________ people.
5 Killer whales often ____________ other mammals, like seals, at night.
6 The man saw the polar bear in the street and ran into a store to ____________.

Polar Bears Are in Town!

Churchill is a small town on the Hudson Bay in Canada. Every October, November, and December, it has some special visitors: polar bears! They can't hunt seals until it is colder and there is more ice, so they visit the town looking for food.

From October to December in 2016, there were 800 people living in Churchill and 10,000 tourists. The tourists were there to see the polar bears – there were more than 1,000 bears.

Some bears attack people, so the police ask people to be careful and to leave their cars open in town. Then people can jump inside if they need to escape an angry bear! To keep people safe, the police sometimes put angry bears in prison for a few days. Then they take them out of the town.

People in the town say the worst year was 1983. On November 29, a young male bear killed a man downtown. This was the first attack for many years. In 2013, a large bear attacked a man in the street. The bear was put in prison and the man went to the doctor, but he was fine after a few days.

4 ☆☆ **Read the article again. Are the sentences *T* (true) or *F* (false)? Correct the false sentences.**

1 Polar bears visit the town every August.
  F. Polar bears visit the town from October to December.
2 The polar bears go to the town because it's colder there.
  ____
3 When the polar bears are angry, people can hide in cars.
  ____
4 The polar bears that attack people go to prison.
  ____

5 ☆☆☆ **Answer the questions with your own ideas.**

1 What do you think the polar bears eat in Churchill?
  ____
2 Do you think the food they eat in Churchill is good for them? Why / Why not?
  ____

GRAMMAR IN ACTION

Simple Past: *To Be, There Was/Were*

1 ☆ Circle the correct options.

1 The polar bears *was* / *were* (circled) in Churchill in November because *there wasn't* (circled) / *there weren't* enough food for them to eat in the river.

2 In the past, the weather *was* / *were* always cold in November, and *there was* / *there were* a lot of ice on the river.

3 When it *was* / *were* colder, *there was* / *there were* seals for the polar bears to eat in the river.

4 In the past, *there was* / *there were* more ice because the temperatures *wasn't* / *weren't* as high.

2 ☆ Match the questions with the answers.

1 Was it hotter in the past? ☐ a Yes, there were.

2 Were they wild animals? ☐ b No, there wasn't.

3 Was there ice in summer? ☐ c Yes, they were.

4 Were there seals? ☐ d No, it wasn't.

3 ☆☆ Complete the text with *was(n't)/were(n't)*.

Thousands of years ago, there were mammoths in Europe. They [1] were large mammals with very big tusks. They [2] ________ very strong. They [3] ________ like the elephants we see today because they [4] ________ much bigger and had fur. The saber-toothed tiger also lived in Europe at the same time. It [5] ________ really a tiger. It [6] ________ a big cat. Its teeth [7] ________ very long, and it [8] ________ a very dangerous animal.

4 ☆☆ Complete the text with the correct form of *there was* or *there were*.

When I was a girl, I lived in South Africa. Around my house, [1] there wasn't a lot to do, but [2] ________ a lot of animals to see because we lived next to a wildlife park. In my bedroom, [3] ________ a big window, and in the mornings, I could see a lot of animals. [4] ________ hippos in the water, and [5] ________ enormous elephants sleeping. [6] ________ always a big giraffe next to a tree and a strange bird sitting on the tree that looked angry! My favorite animals are tigers, but [7] ________ any tigers in the wildlife park. That's because there aren't any tigers in South Africa. [8] ________ a lot of time to see the animals because I was at school all day, but I remember all of them.

5 ☆☆ Put the words in the correct order to complete the questions. Then write answers for you in your notebook.

1 were / Where / on Saturday / you / ?

Where were you on Saturday?

2 your / favorite / six / animal / when / you / were / ?

What was ________________________

3 people / were / there / last year / your / class / in / ?

How many ________________________

4 in / 2011 / were / you / ?

How old ________________________

5 your town / in / were / you / when / young / a zoo / ?

Was there ________________________

6 ☆☆☆ Find out about an animal from the past, like mammoths or saber-toothed tigers. Write three sentences about them. Use *was* and *were*.

____

____

____

VOCABULARY AND LISTENING

Adjectives

1 ☆ **Choose the correct letters to complete the adjectives.**

a c d ~~f~~ g i l m n r u y

1 beauti*f*ul	5 heav__	9 ti__y
2 s__art	6 l__zy	10 la__ge
3 __ute	7 wil__	11 q__iet
4 dan__erous	8 no__sy	12 __ong

2 ☆☆ **Complete the text with adjectives from Exercise 1.**

I have a [1] *beautiful* little cat. He has a pretty face, and I think he's really [2] __________. He's [3] __________, too, and can do a lot of tricks. My mom likes him because he doesn't make a lot of noise like some pets. She says he's very [4] __________. He can't run fast because his legs aren't very [5] __________! I prefer small pets because some of my friends' big pets are [6] __________, and they make me nervous.

3 ☆☆☆ **Which pets do your family or friends have? Use the adjectives and your own ideas to write four sentences.**

My best friend has a tiny mouse.

____

____

____

____

A Class Discussion

7.01 **4** ☆ **Listen to a teacher talking about wolves with her class. Circle the correct answers.**

1 The teacher is talking about wolves that live in an *American park* / *English zoo*.

2 There weren't any wolves there for *50* / *100* years.

3 There were about *6* / *100* wolves there last year.

7.01 **5** ☆☆ **Listen again and answer the questions. Remember the *Learn to Learn* tip: look for the question words and think about the answers before you listen.**

1 How does one student describe wolves?

They are fast, dangerous, and smart.

2 Why weren't there any wolves in Yellowstone Park for 100 years?

____

____

3 How many wolves were in the park about 25 years ago?

____

____

4 Why was it difficult for the wolves at first?

____

____

5 Why is it difficult to see wolves in the park?

____

____

6 ☆☆☆ **Which other wild animals do you think live in Yellowstone Park? Write some ideas below.**

____

____

____

____

____

GRAMMAR IN ACTION

Simple Past: Regular and Irregular Verbs

1 ★ Write the infinitive of these past tense verbs.

1 had *have*	5 heard ______	9 shared ______
2 slept ______	6 saw ______	10 wanted ______
3 took ______	7 became ______	11 found ______
4 looked ______	8 gave ______	12 went ______

2 ★★ Complete the sentences with the correct simple past form of the verbs in the box.

look ~~not give~~ have not want
sleep not find see not go

1 You *didn't give* the donkey its food.
2 We ______ a lot of snakes at the wildlife park.
3 The horse ______ to eat my apple. It wasn't hungry.
4 They ______ for the cat in the yard, but they ______ him.
5 My dad ______ a parrot as a pet when he was a child.
6 The cat ______ out. She ______ on my bed all day.

3 ★★ Write the words in the correct order to make sentences.

1 park / years / The / 20 / safari / opened / ago
The safari park opened 20 years ago.
2 Crocodiles / killed / year / 1,000 / people / last
______
3 bears / days / in town / ago, / Two / three / were / there
______
4 blue / last / saw / whales / summer / They
______
5 an / The / home / hour / cat / came / ago
______

4 ★★★ Complete the text with the simple past form of the verbs in parentheses.

Flo, a dog from Northern Ireland, disappeared in October 2011. The Gallaghers, Flo's family, 1 *looked* (look) for her, but they 2 ______ (not find) her. They were very sad. Then in 2014, a volunteer at the local animal hospital 3 ______ (hear) about a dog with no home. The dog 4 ______ (sleep) in an old building about ten miles from the Gallaghers' house. The volunteers at the hospital 5 ______ (not want) the dog to stay there. They 6 ______ (go) to find her. Soon the dog 7 ______ (have) a new home at the animal hospital, and they 8 ______ (share) photos of her on Facebook. The Gallagher family 9 ______ (see) the photos and 10 ______ (become) very excited – it was Flo! The next day they 11 ______ (take) her home. They 12 ______ (give) her a big dinner.

WRITING

A Biography

1 ★ **Look at the photos and read the biography. Which animals did Jack help?**

____

Jack Oliver

1 Jack Oliver was born in Australia [1]*in* / *on* 1978. His family started an animal sanctuary to give animals a safe place to live. [2]*When* / *At* Jack was five, he found a three-meter snake in his yard! It was injured! Jack and his parents decided to take care of it. Jack helped at the sanctuary, and he became an animal expert.

2 Jack met his wife Alison [3]*on* / *in* 2003. They had a daughter named Ava. [4]*In* / *On* 2005, Jack started to make TV shows with a local TV channel. He filmed several series at his family's sanctuary. He also went to other countries to find and help injured animals. He helped to make them better and find a safe place for them to live. [5]*In* / *On* September 25, 2012, Jack had an accident with a crocodile, but he survived.

3 Jack's wife and daughter help with his work. A few weeks [6]*when* / *ago*, Ava found an injured duck and decided to take it to her father's sanctuary. She helped her father to take care of it. Ava wants to be an animal expert one day, just like her father!

2 ★★ **Circle the correct prepositions (1–6) in the biography.**

3 ★★ **Read the biography again and write the events in the box in the timeline below.**

~~born~~	crocodile attack	found a snake
met Alison	TV shows	

1978	1983	2003	2005	2012
1 born	2 ________	3 ________	4 ________	5 ________

4 ★★ **Match headings a–c with paragraphs 1–3.**

a Now ☐
b Early life ☐
c Main events ☐

PLAN

5 ★★ **Write a biography about a famous person who works with animals. Look for information on the Internet and create a timeline about his or her life. Use Exercise 3 to help you.**

6 **Decide what information to include in each paragraph. Use Exercise 4 to help you.**

WRITE

7 ★★★ **Write your biography. Remember to include three paragraphs, the simple past, and time expressions, and the *Useful Language* expressions (see Student's Book, p89).**

CHECK

8 **Do you ...**

- give information from the timeline of your famous person?
- write about the events in their life in the correct order?

7 REVIEW

VOCABULARY

1 Complete the crossword. Use the pictures.

ACROSS →

DOWN ↓

2 Complete the sentences with an adjective from the box.

beautiful cute dangerous heavy large lazy noisy quiet smart tiny wild

1 Kodiak brown bears are very ___________ animals, but their babies are ___________ – they are only about 23 cm long, and they weigh only 450 g.

2 Hippos are very ___________ animals. They kill a lot of people.

3 My snake doesn't make much noise. He is very ___________.

4 When blue whales are born, they weigh about 2,700 kg. That's ___________!

5 Male lions are ___________. They sleep, and the female lions hunt.

6 African gray parrots can learn 1,000 words. They are really ___________.

7 Howler monkeys are very ___________. You can hear them from 4 km away!

8 Baby lions look ___________, but be careful! They are ___________ animals, not pets, and can attack you.

9 Oh, I love looking at photos of tigers! I think tigers are really ___________ animals.

GRAMMAR IN ACTION

3 Circle the correct options in the conversation.

A [1]*Was / Were* you at school yesterday?

B No, I [2]*wasn't / weren't*. [3]*There were / I was* on a school field trip to an aquarium.

A [4]*Was it / Was there* good?

B It was fantastic! There [5]*was / were* hundreds of different fish. My favorites [6]*were / was* the parrot fish and the clown fish. [7]*There was / It was* a dolphin area, too.

A [8]*Were there / There was* any sharks?

B Yes, [9]*they were / there were*, but there [10]*wasn't / weren't* time to go and see them. The aquarium's really big!

4 Complete the text with the simple past form of the verbs in parentheses.

Last year, I [1]________ (want) a pet, but I [2]________ (not have) a lot of money, so I [3]________ (go) to an animal rescue center. At the center, I [4]________ (see) a lot of animals, but I [5]________ (not know) which one I [6]________ (like) best. Then I [7]________ (hear) a noise in a corner. A tiny white cat [8]________ (look) up at me with his big blue eyes. He was really cute. I [9]________ (take) him home, and he [10]________ (become) my best friend.

CUMULATIVE GRAMMAR

5 Complete the conversation with the missing words. Circle the correct options.

ISA Hi, Adela! How [1]________ your weekend?

ADELA [2]________ really nice, thanks! On Saturday morning I [3]________ basketball with my team – we [4]________ our game.

ISA No way! Your team always wins!

ADELA I know, but it [5]________ fun to play, and we are still at the top of the league table. Anyway, on Saturday afternoon I [6]________ to a soccer match with my cousins and my uncle – my team [7]________ so I [8]________ really happy!

ISA Wow! Lucky you!

ADELA Yes, then on Sunday afternoon, I [9]________ my friends, and we went to the movies. [10]________ a great movie! The best part was the burger we [11]________ in a restaurant near the theater after the movie. It was delicious!

ISA Really? Where's the restaurant?

ADELA On George Street. Let's go there now!

1	a was	b are	c were
2	a There was	b There were	c It was
3	a plays	b did play	c played
4	a lost	b losed	c loses
5	a were	b weren't	c was
6	a was	b go	c went
7	a wins	b won	c win
8	a wasn't	b aren't	c was
9	a meet	b meeted	c met
10	a It was	b It weren't	c It wasn't
11	a eat	b eated	c ate

8 What did you find?

VOCABULARY
Places in Town

1 ☆ **Look at the photos and complete the words for places.**

1 s w i m m i n g
p o o l

2 b _ _ _ _ _ _ _
a _ _ _ _

3 p _ _ _
o _ _ _ _ _

4 g _ _

5 a _ _ _ _ _ _ _ _

6 h _ _ _ _ _ _ _

7 s _ _ _ _ _ _ _
m _ _ _

8 p _ _ _ _ _ _
l _ _

9 m _ _ _ _
t _ _ _ _ _ _

10 i _ _ r _ _ _

11 s _ _ _ _ _
p _ _ _

2 ☆ **Look at the words in Exercise 1. How many are compound nouns?** ________

3 ☆ **Write a place from Exercise 1.**

1 I went there when I fell off my bike. hospital
2 It was cold in there, but we wore gloves and it was fun! ________
3 We went there to buy some clothes and gifts. ________
4 I went there to send a letter. ________

4 ☆☆ **Complete the text with the places from Exercise 1.**

My friend Edie lives in a small town. She always goes to the city to buy her clothes because there isn't a [1] shopping mall in her town. There's a library with a lot of good books, and a [2] ________ to send letters, but nothing else. There isn't a [3] ________ to watch movies! I live in a big town, and there's everything we need. I go to the [4] ________ to play tennis and take swimming classes at the [5] ________. In December, I love ice skating at the [6] ________ and going bowling at the [7] ________. My town also has a [8] ________ – I was there last year when I broke my arm! But my favorite place is downtown – it's an [9] ________ with a lot of fish. My dad takes me there sometimes and leaves the car in a big [10] ________. After that, I usually go skateboarding in a cool [11] ________ nearby.

Explore It!

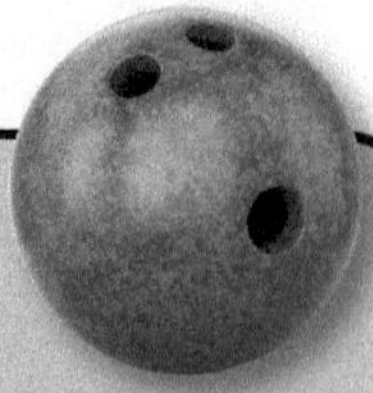

Guess the correct answer.

The first bowling alley opened in …

a London in 1889. b New York in 1840.

Find another interesting fact about a place from Exercise 1 in your country. Write a question and send it to a classmate in an email, or ask them it in the next class.

READING

An Online Travel Article

1 ☆ **Look at the photos and read the article. Which photo (1–3) is the article not about?** ________

2 ☆☆ **Read the article and underline these words. Check their meaning in a dictionary and then complete the sentences.**

believe	belong	case
~~scuba diving~~	social media	

1 I love swimming, but I prefer scuba diving underwater.
2 Matt has a blog and shares his videos on ________.
3 I can't ________ it! Our birthdays are on the same day!
4 Keep the camera safe. Put it in its ________.
5 This cap isn't mine. Does it ________ to you?

3 ☆☆ **Read the article again. Put the events in the correct order (1–8).**

a Serina saw the photos on social media. ☐
b Serina went scuba diving. 1
c The teacher put a message on social media. ☐
d The teacher looked at the photos on the camera. ☐
e Some children found a camera on the beach. ☐
f Serina lost her camera. ☐
g The children and their teacher took the camera back to school. ☐
h Thousands of people shared the message. ☐

4 ☆☆☆ **Imagine you are Serina. Write a thank-you note to Mr. Park Lee and his class. Write at least four sentences.**

Dear Mr. Park Lee and students: …

1

2

3

Lost Under the Ocean

In March 2018, a class from Mount Elementary School in Su'ao, Taiwan, went to clean the beach. They found a camera in an underwater case. They didn't know it was a camera at first because the case had things from the ocean all over it. They showed their teacher, Mr. Park Lee. He opened the case. Inside was a digital camera, and no sea water!

The class took the camera back to school. Everyone had questions: Did it work? Were there any photos in it? Did it belong to someone from Su'ao? Could they find him or her? The camera worked! Mr. Park Lee looked at the photos. They showed fish and people underwater, and streets in Japan. Mr. Lee put some photos with a message in Chinese and Japanese on social media. He asked people to share the message with their friends. In the next 24 hours, thousands of people saw the message. One of them was Serina Tsubakihara, a Japanese student. She couldn't believe it – they were her photos!

Serina went scuba diving near Okinawa, in Japan, in September 2015. She lost her camera there. It was in the ocean for more than two years and traveled 250 kilometers to Taiwan!

GRAMMAR IN ACTION

Simple Past: Questions

1 ★ **Match questions 1–5 with answers a–e.**

1 Did Sam find his hat? c
2 Did the students go to the bowling alley? ☐
3 Did you and Dana finish your project? ☐
4 Did the ice rink close at six o'clock? ☐
5 Did Rosa go to the movies? ☐

a Yes, we did.
b No, she didn't.
c Yes, he did.
d Yes, it did.
e No, they didn't.

2 ★ **Answer the questions for you. Mark (✓) the correct column.**

Yesterday, did you …	Yes, I did.	No, I didn't.
… have a big breakfast?		
… play any sports?		
… go to the movies?		
… visit a family member?		
… hang out with friends after school?		

3 ★★ **Write the words in the correct order to make simple past questions.**

1 Alex / to / post office / Did / go / the / ?
Did Alex go to the post office?
2 buy / a / Clara / bag / new / Did / ?
____
3 Did / time / they / good / have / a / ?
____
4 aquarium / the / Did / enjoy / you / ?
____
5 your / Did / to / parents / walk / restaurant / the / ?
____

4 ★★ **Write simple past questions. Do you know the answers?**

1 Shakespeare / write *Romeo and Juliet* / ?
Did Shakespeare write Romeo and Juliet?
2 Marie Curie / win a Nobel Prize / ?
____
3 Picasso / paint the *Mona Lisa* / ?
____
4 Columbus / discover Australia / ?
____
5 Emma Watson / work in the movie *Frozen* / ?
____

5 ★★★ **Complete the conversation with simple past questions. Use the words in parentheses and the underlined verbs.**

MOM Hi! [1] Did you have a good match? (you / good match)
RYAN No, we <u>had</u> a terrible match.
MOM Oh, no! [2] ____________ ? (your team)
RYAN Yes. We <u>lost</u> 5–3.
MOM [3] ____________ (you / a goal)
RYAN No, I didn't <u>score</u> this time.
MOM What about Henry? [4] ____________ ? (he)
RYAN No, he didn't <u>play</u>. He fell off his skateboard the other day.
MOM Oh, no. [5] ____________ ? (he / anything)
RYAN Luckily, he didn't <u>break</u> his leg. He just hurt it.
MOM Good! [6] ____________ after the match? (you / a snack)
RYAN Yes, I <u>had</u> some chocolate. That was the best part!

VOCABULARY AND LISTENING

Personal Possessions

1 ★ Complete the definitions with the words in the box.

bus pass camera ~~headphones~~ ID card keys money passport phone portable charger

We use …

1 _headphones_ to listen to music.
2 our _______ and _______ to show who we are.
3 _______ to buy things.
4 _______ to open a door.
5 a _______ to travel on public transportation.
6 a _______ to text or talk to someone.
7 a _______ to take photos or make videos.
8 a _______ to keep our phone, tablet, or laptop working.

2 ★★ Complete the text with words from Exercise 1.

Home News Blog Lifestyle

I had a bad day on Tuesday. I couldn't take the bus home because I couldn't find my [1] _bus pass_. Then I couldn't get into our apartment because I didn't have my [2] _______. I used my [3] _______ to text my mom, but she was at the doctor's! I went to the library to do some homework on my laptop, but it had no battery power and the [4] _______ was at home. I had some [5] _______ in my pocket, so I bought a drink at the café.

My sister loses things, too. Last July, she lost her [6] _______ on vacation and couldn't take any photos. Then she left her [7] _______ on a bus, so she couldn't listen to music on her phone. What a family!

A Radio Interview

8.01 3 ★ Look at the photos and answer the questions with your own ideas. Then listen and check your answers.

1 What did Sabina lose? _______
2 Where did she find it/them? _______

8.01 4 ★★ Listen again. Underline and correct one mistake in each sentence.

1 The tickets weren't Sabina's birthday present. _were_
2 Sabina asked her mom for help. _______
3 Sabina's friend put the envelope in the trash can. _______
4 Sabina's CD wasn't in her room. _______
5 She didn't go to the concert. _______

8.01 5 ★★ Listen again and complete the sentences.

1 The radio show today is about _______.
2 Sabina's best friend never _______.
3 The questions helped Sabina _______.

GRAMMAR IN ACTION

Simple Past: *Wh-* Questions

1 ☆ **Complete the questions with the question words in the box.**

How much What When ~~Where~~ Who

1 A: ___Where___ did you buy your new headphones? B: Around the corner.
2 A: ___________ did they cost? B: About $20.
3 A: ___________ did you do last weekend? B: I went to the movies.
4 A: ___________ did you go with? B: My cousin.
5 A: ___________ did you get that camera? B: Last week, for my birthday.

2 ☆☆ **Write simple past questions. Then match them with answers a–e.**

1 What / you / do / last night? [e]
What did you do last night?
2 How / you / get / to school / today? [ ]
____
3 Who / you / sit / with in class / yesterday? [ ]
____
4 Where / you / go / last weekend? [ ]
____
5 What time / get up / on Sunday? [ ]
____

a My best friend.
b Really late! At 11 o'clock!
c I caught the bus.
d I went to the aquarium with my friends.
e ~~I watched TV and read a book.~~

3 ☆☆☆ **Complete questions in the conversation with the simple past. Use the answers to help you.**

ANA Hey! I went to a baseball game in Chicago.
ROB Wow! When [1] ___*did you go*___?
ANA I went last weekend, on Saturday.
ROB Who [2] ___________?
ANA I went with my family and my American cousin, Martin.
ROB Who [3] ___________?
ANA I sat with Martin. He told me everything about the game.
ROB What [4] ___________?
ANA I ate a big burger!
ROB How [5] ___________?
ANA We went home by bus.
ROB What time [6] ___________?
ANA I can't remember, but I know we got home really late!

4 ☆☆☆ **Think about an interesting event you went to. Write the questions. Then answer them.**

1 where / go? *Where did you go?*
2 when / go? ___________
3 who / go with? ___________
4 how / feel? ___________

I went ... ___________
____
____
____

WRITING

A Blog Post

1 ☆ **Read the blog post. What problem started Bruno's bad day? Circle the correct answer.**

a His camera didn't work.

b His sister's camera didn't work.

c His parents' car didn't work.

HOME | ABOUT ME | ARCHIVE | FOLLOW

BRUNO'S BIG BLOG

A Bad Day on the Weekend

1 Last Saturday, it was my sister's birthday. We gave her a camera, but it didn't work. My mom and dad decided to go to the shopping mall to exchange it, so we all got ready.

2 When we got into the car, it didn't work, so we decided to take the bus. But it got worse! It started raining, so we arrived wet and cold at the store. Awful.

3 At the store, the sales assistant asked for the receipt to exchange the camera, and guess what? My parents didn't have it … so my dad went back home to get it. After an hour, he came back, and my sister got her new camera.

4 It was lunchtime, and we were really hungry, so we had lunch in the shopping mall. But when my parents wanted to pay, they couldn't find their wallets … they were at home!

5 When did you have a bad day on a weekend? What happened? Tell me!

2 ☆☆ **Read the blog again. Put the events in the correct order (1–5).**

a Bruno's dad went back home. ☐

b They needed a receipt for the camera. ☐

c They took the bus to the shopping mall. ☐

d The family car didn't work. 1

e Bruno's parents couldn't pay for lunch. ☐

3 ☆☆ **Join the sentences with *so*.**

1 It was my sister's birthday. We bought her a phone.

It was my sister's birthday, so we bought her a phone.

2 The phone didn't work. We decided to exchange it.

____

3 My dad showed the receipt. My sister got her new phone.

____

4 My parents couldn't find their wallets. They couldn't pay for lunch.

____

4 Read the blog post again. Match topics a–e with paragraphs 1–5.

a what happened next ☐

b what day it was and how it started 1

c what happened later ☐

d sign off and ask questions ☐

e the end of the bad day ☐

PLAN

5 ☆☆ **Write a blog post about a bad day on the weekend. Make notes about your bad day. Think about the answers to these questions.**

When did the bad day start?
What problems did you and your family/friends have?
When and where did each problem happen?
What did you do? What did the other people do?
How did you feel?

6 Decide what information to include in each paragraph. Use the information in Exercise 4 to help you.

WRITE

7 ☆☆☆ **Write your blog post. Remember to include four paragraphs, the simple past for the questions at the end, and the expressions from the *Useful Language* box (see Student's Book, p101).**

CHECK

8 Do you …

- use a title for your blog post?
- use *so* to join ideas and explain the results?
- say how you felt on your bad day?

8 REVIEW

VOCABULARY

1 Where did Tim go last week? Match the sentences with the words in the box. (Circle) the four extra words.

aquarium bowling alley gym hospital ice rink movie theater parking lot post office shopping mall skate park swimming pool

1 He mailed a letter to Ben. ______________
2 He saw a basketball game. ______________
3 He visited his sick uncle. ______________
4 He saw an amazing movie. ______________
5 He bought a new pair of jeans. ______________
6 He saw a lot of dolphins! ______________
7 He dived into the water. ______________

2 Which four places from Exercise 1 didn't Tim go to?

______________ ______________

______________ ______________

3 Complete the sentences with the words in the box.

camera concert tickets headphones keys money passport phone tablet

1 I don't have any ______________ to buy a drink.
2 You need your ______________ to travel to a different country.
3 These ______________ don't work. I can't hear anything!
4 These days, everyone has a ______________ to text and call people.
5 It's easy to use a ______________. You just touch the screen and it works!
6 Let's buy ______________ to see Katy Perry.
7 Henry doesn't use his phone to take photos. He uses his ______________.
8 Where are the ______________ to open the door?

GRAMMAR IN ACTION

4 Complete the questions and short answers with the simple past. Use the verbs in parentheses.

ASHLEY 1 ________ you ________ (go) to the bowling alley yesterday, Max?
MAX Yes, I 2 ________.
ASHLEY 3 ________ you ________ (meet) Maddie there?
MAX No, I 4 ________. I was with Alex and Elena.
ASHLEY Cool! And 5 ________ you ________ (have) a good time?
MAX No, we 6 ________. Alex dropped the bowling ball on his foot!
ASHLEY Oh, no! Poor Alex! 7 ________ his parents ________ (take) him to the hospital?
MAX Yes, they 8 ________.
ASHLEY Was his foot OK? 9 ________ he ________ (break) it?
MAX No, he 10 ________. He was very lucky!

5 Write simple past questions.

1 What / you / do / last night? ______________________

2 How / your dad / get to work / this morning? ______________________

3 What time / you / get home / after school? ______________________

4 Who / you / see / yesterday? ______________________

5 Where / you / go / last weekend? ______________________

6 How / you / feel / after the exam? ______________________

CUMULATIVE GRAMMAR

6 Complete the conversation with the missing words. Circle the correct options.

BRENDA Hi, Theo. Where 1 ______________ go yesterday?

THEO I 2 ______________ to the ice rink to watch my brother.

BRENDA 3 ______________ go ice skating, too?

THEO No! I don't 4 ______________ ice skating. I think it's dangerous!

BRENDA Yes, me too! The first time I 5 ______________ it, I nearly 6 ______________ my leg!

THEO The other problem is that 7 ______________ usually a lot of people on the ice.

BRENDA Yes, you're right! 8 ______________ does your brother go?

THEO He 9 ______________ every week for about three hours. He says he wants to be the 10 ______________ ice skater in town!

BRENDA 11 ______________ you at the ice rink all day yesterday?

THEO Yes, but he 12 ______________ me out for dinner afterward!

1	a do you	b did you	c you did
2	a go	b went	c goes
3	a Did you	b You	c Were you
4	a like	b likes	c liked
5	a try	b tries	c tried
6	a broke	b break	c breaks
7	a there is	b there are	c there were
8	a How often	b How many	c How
9	a practice	b practices	c practiced
10	a good	b better	c best
11	a Did	b Was	c Were
12	a take	b took	c takes

9 What makes a great vacation?

VOCABULARY
Outdoor Life

1 ★ Look at the pictures. Complete the activities with the words and phrases in the box.

a compass	a fire	a map	a shelter	fish	~~food and water~~	fruit	over a campfire	plants	wood

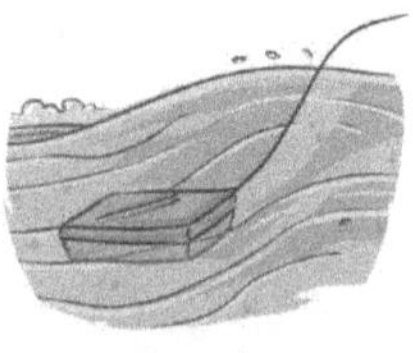

1 find food and water

6 cook ______

2 pick ______

7 identify ______

3 light ______

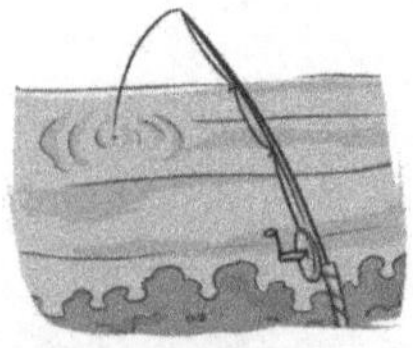

8 catch ______

4 collect ______

9 build ______

5 use ______

10 read ______

2 ★★ Match the sentences with activities from Exercise 1.

a You do this before nighttime. You sleep there. [9]
b You need to do this before you light a fire. [ ]
c You need to find trees with apples, pears, etc. to do this. [ ]
d You use this to see where places are. [ ]
e You use this to know which way to go. [ ]
f You do this to keep warm and to cook. [ ]
g You do this when you are hungry or thirsty. [ ]

3 ★★ Complete the text with the correct form of the verbs from Exercise 1.

I often go to the mountains with my family. When we get there, some of us ¹ collect wood for the fire and others ² ______ a shelter. Next, we all go to ³ ______ water and ⁴ ______ fish for lunch. My dad always ⁵ ______ the fish over a campfire. It can take a long time to ⁶ ______ the fire if the wood is wet. In the afternoon, we go for a walk to ⁷ ______ plants. I write their names in my notebook. We sometimes ⁸ ______ fruit, too. We ⁹ ______ a compass in the mountains because it's easy to get lost!

4 ★★★ Write about one or more outdoor activities that you do on vacation. Look at Exercise 3 to help you.

______

______

______

______

Explore It!

Guess the correct answer.

In this country, students have the longest summer break from school in Europe. They get 13 weeks! Which country is it?

a Italy b Germany c Portugal

Find another interesting fact about how people spend their free time in your country. Write a question and send it to a classmate in an email, or ask them it in the next class.

READING
A Pamphlet

ADVENTURE TRIPS

FIND AN ADVENTURE TRIP FOR YOU THIS SUMMER!

You'll learn new things and have a lot of fun! Join us on one of our three Adventure Trips. Read and choose the best one for you!

1. WHITE WATER KAYAKING TRIP (THREE DAYS)

Day 1: Meet your instructors and practice on white water.

Day 2: Learn how to use a compass and choose the best part of the river for your kayak.

Day 3: Follow the fast water and show your instructors how good you are!

We'll also teach you to build a shelter and help you collect wood for a campfire.

2. MOUNTAIN CLIMBING TRIP (FIVE DAYS)

Days 1–2: Walk five kilometers in the mountains each day with your guide. Learn how to identify plants and pick the right fruit to eat!

Days 3–5: Spend three days mountain climbing. Learn how to read a map and help each other.

You won't get much time to sit down! But you'll become the best mountain climber!

3. WATER AND COUNTRY TRIP (SIX DAYS)

Day 1: Learn how to catch fish in the river and then cook them over a campfire!

Days 2–3: Travel along the river in a kayak and work as a team.

Days 4–6: Leave the water to go horseback riding in the country with your guides!

You won't be bored on this trip. We'll play fun games, and you'll make good friends!

WHAT ARE YOU WAITING FOR?

CHOOSE THE BEST ADVENTURE TRIP FOR YOU!

You'll learn new sports and skills, meet new people, and have a great time!

For more information and booking details, visit our website.

We'll give you breakfast and lunch, but sometimes … you'll need to find your own dinner!

1 ★ **Read the pamphlet. Then complete the sentences with the phrases in the box.**

mountain climbing	water and country	white water kayaking

1 You can learn how to read a map and identify plants on the __________ trip.

2 You can learn how to cook your own food over a campfire on the __________ trip.

3 You can learn how to use a compass on the __________ trip.

2 ★★ **Read the pamphlet again and underline these words. Then check their meaning in a dictionary and complete the sentences.**

white water	~~river~~	follow	guides	spend

1 There are a lot of fish in that _river_.

2 The water in a river that moves very quickly is called __________.

3 Our mountain __________ showed us some good places to climb.

4 Don't walk alone in the forest. Always __________ the instructor.

5 I need to __________ more time learning how to build a shelter!

3 ★★★ **Answer the questions.**

1 On Trip 1, who do you meet on Day 1?
your instructors

2 On which day do you use a compass?
____

3 On Trip 2, how far do you walk on Day 1?
____

4 What things can you learn on Trip 2?
____

5 On Trip 3, when do you do water activities?
____

4 ★★★ **Answer the questions with your own ideas.**

1 Which trip is the most exciting? Why?
____

2 Which trip is the most difficult? Why?
____

GRAMMAR IN ACTION

Future with *Will/Won't*

1 ★ Circle the correct options.

1 The climbing trip *be* / *will be* a lot of fun. It *not will* / *won't* be boring.

2 We *won't* / *not will* make our own lunch. The instructors *make will* / *will make* it.

3 A: *Will you* / *You will* go on the kayaking trip?
B: Yes, *I'll* / *I will*.

4 A: *Will* / *Will not* the instructors make dinner for you?
B: No, they *not will* / *won't*.

2 ★★ Write sentences with *I'll* or *I won't*.

1 (✓) learn how to catch fish
I'll learn how to catch fish.

2 (✗) get bored
______

3 (✓) go in a kayak
______

4 (✗) stay for two weeks
______

5 (✓) walk six kilometers
______

6 (✓) cook food over a campfire
______

3 ★★ Complete the email with the correct form of *will* and the verbs in parentheses.

Hi Victoria,

I got back a few hours ago from my family camping trip. It was OK, but my sister says she [1] won't go (not go) again. She also [2] ______ (not sleep) in a shelter again! She says she [3] ______ (go) with her friends on a beach vacation because it [4] ______ (be) sunny and they [5] ______ (not do) anything all day - just sleep and swim! She's 18 now, so I guess we [6] ______ (not be) together next summer. I [7] ______ (miss) her! How was your vacation?

4 ★★ Write the words in the correct order to make questions. Then answer the questions for you in your notebook.

1 with your family / Will / this year / you / go on vacation / ?
Will you go on vacation with your family this year?

2 you / Will / see / on the weekend / your best friend / ?
______

3 tomorrow / will / you / do / What / ?
______

4 this summer / go / you / Where / will / ?
______

5 will / you / Who / next week / see / ?
______

6 go shopping / you / Will / tomorrow / ?
______

5 ★★★ You are going on one of the adventure trips from the pamphlet on p73. Make four predictions about it with *will/won't*.

1 I'll make new friends.

2 ______

3 ______

4 ______

5 ______

VOCABULARY AND LISTENING

Vacations

1 ☆ **Complete the accommodation words in the spidergram with the missing vowels.**

VACATIONS

- 1 a p a rtm e nt
- 2 b__ __d & br__ __kf__st
- 3 c__mp__r
- 4 r__s__rt
- 5 r__cr__ __t__ __n__l v__h__cl__
- 6 c__b__n
- 7 h__t__l
- 8 t__nt
- 9 y__ __th h__st__l

2 ☆☆ **Complete the text with words from Exercise 1.**

My family and I want to go on vacation, but everyone wants to stay in a different place! My dad wants to stay in a [1]hotel________, but my mom prefers a [2]b________ & b________. My brother loves moving from place to place, so he thinks a [3]r________ v________ is perfect! My grandma wants a little house like a [4]c________, but my dad says that's very small. My aunt showed me a picture of an amazing city [5]a________. It looks great, but I want to stay in a [6]y________ h________ – it's the best place to make friends!

A Conversation

3 9.01 ☆ **Listen to the conversation. Where will the girls spend their summer vacations? Circle the correct answer.**

a in a cabin b at home c in Canada

4 9.01 ☆☆ **Listen again. Match the phrases with the people in the box.**

aunt and uncle	Camila	~~parents~~	Tara

1 on vacation in another country ____parents____
2 a lot of fun ________
3 at home with her parents in the summer ________
4 invites her friend to do an outdoor activity ________

5 9.01 ☆☆ **Listen again and answer the questions.**

1 How will Camila's parents travel around Canada?
in an RV
2 Who will be with Camila for two weeks?
____
3 Whose parents have a vacation cabin?
____
4 What will Tara's parents do in July and August?
____
5 Why does Camila ask Tara to stay with her?
____
6 Why doesn't Tara like camping?
____

6 ☆☆☆ **Your parents are going on vacation, and you will stay at home with someone else from your family. Make a spidergram with positive/negative things about this.**

GRAMMAR IN ACTION

Present Continuous for Future

1 ☆ **Match 1–6 with a–f.**

1 My mom's working on Saturday. [c]
2 Are you watching the match tomorrow? [ ]
3 Mario isn't playing tennis after school. [ ]
4 Are your cousins arriving soon? [ ]
5 We're going on a field trip tomorrow. [ ]
6 How are you getting to the gym? [ ]

a We're visiting a museum.
b My dad's driving me.
c ~~She's going to a meeting~~.
d He's going to the dentist.
e No, I'm not. I'm studying.
f Yes, they are. On Sunday.

2 ☆☆ **Write sentences with the present continuous.**

1 We / go / to the beach / on the weekend
We're going to the beach on the weekend.
2 Debra / not have / a birthday party / this year
______
3 My grandparents / fly / to Italy / in August
______
4 you / have / lunch / at a restaurant / on Sunday / ?
______
5 We / not do / anything special / this weekend
______
6 How / she / get / to work / today / ?
______

3 ☆☆ **Complete the conversation with the present continuous form of the verbs in parentheses.**

CARLA What [1] *are you doing* (you / do) in the summer?
NICO In July, I [2] ______ (go) to a summer camp in the mountains.
CARLA That sounds fun! [3] ______ (you / sleep) in a tent?
NICO No, I [4] ______ (not camp). We [5] ______ (stay) in cabins.
CARLA What [6] ______ (your parents / do)?
NICO They [7] ______ (start) their vacation in August. They [8] ______ (meet) me at the summer camp, and we [9] ______ (drive) across the country in an RV.

Be Going To

4 ☆ **Underline and correct one mistake in each sentence.**

1 <u>We going</u> to visit the water park. *We're going*
2 Are you going see the new movie? ______
3 I'm not go to buy a camera. ______
4 They're going living in the country. ______
5 Mia isn't to go swimming after school. ______
6 Leo going to learn to skateboard. ______

5 ☆☆☆ **Write questions with the present continuous or *be going to*. Then answer the questions for you.**

1 What / do / this weekend? (present continuous)
What are you doing this weekend?
______
2 What / do / tonight? (present continuous)
______
______
3 What TV shows / watch / this week? (*be going to*)
______
______
4 How / celebrate / your birthday / this year? (*be going to*)
______
______

WRITING

An Email

1 ☆ **Read the email. How does Paige know Ava?**

____

2 ☆☆ **Circle the correct prepositions (1–10) in the email.**

Hi Ava,

1 Thanks for your email. I'm really excited you're coming to stay with us in New Zealand [1]*on* / *in* January! We'll have a great time! You'll enjoy Mission Bay and seeing our friends from elementary school again.

2 Here are the arrangements. [2]*On* / *In* Friday, Mom and I are meeting you [3]*at* / *on* the airport in Auckland. Then we're going to have a night [4]*in* / *at* home, and my dad's cooking. You're sleeping with me [5]*in* / *at* my room. We can talk about your new life in Australia and compare our schools!

3 [6]*In* / *On* Saturday, we're going to the beach. It'll be hot, so we'll go swimming. Hayley, Lily, and Ryan from our elementary school are coming, too! [7]*In* / *On* the evening, we're going to have dinner [8]*on* / *at* my favorite restaurant. Then [9]*on* / *at* Sunday, we're going to Te Urewera National Park for four days. We're staying [10]*in* / *on* a nice cabin. There are beautiful lakes and birds. What do you think?

4 It'll be great to see you again! Is there anything you would like to do? Let me know!

See you soon,

Paige XX

3 **Match topics a–d with paragraphs 1–4.**

a end the email [4]
b respond to your friend's last email [ ]
c describe the first day [ ]
d describe the weekend [ ]

4 ☆☆ **Read the email again. Are the sentences *T* (true) or *F* (false)?**

1 Ava is traveling to Auckland by car. F
2 Ava and Paige are sleeping in the same room. ___
3 They're spending one day at the beach. ___
4 They're having dinner at home on Saturday evening. ___
5 At Te Urewera National Park, they're not staying in a hotel. ___

PLAN

5 ☆☆ **Write an email to a friend from elementary school about plans for their visit. Your friend now lives in another place and is coming to stay with you. Make notes about these things for your email:**

your arrangements
things you intend to do
predictions about what will happen
the place where you are meeting them

6 ☆☆ **Decide what information to include in each paragraph. Use the information in Exercise 3 to help you.**

WRITE

7 ☆☆☆ **Write your email. Remember to include four paragraphs, *will*, *be going to*, and the present continuous for future, and expressions from the *Useful Language* box (see Student's Book, p113).**

CHECK

8 **Do you ...**

- include an arrangement and a prediction for the weekend and the week ahead?
- make predictions about what will or won't happen?
- tell your friend where you are going to meet them?

9 REVIEW

VOCABULARY

1 Circle the correct verb.

1 *catch* / *build* a shelter
2 *light* / *cook* a fire
3 *build* / *pick* fruit
4 *catch* / *light* fish
5 *use* / *cook* over a campfire
6 *collect* / *build* wood
7 *read* / *collect* a map
8 *build* / *identify* plants

2 Find nine words for accommodation in the word search. Then match them with sentences 1–9 below.

C	T	E	N	T	Y	B	E	G	F	B
A	B	R	L	H	O	C	I	J	N	E
M	C	E	O	I	U	E	O	G	C	D
P	A	S	M	K	T	G	U	B	T	&
E	I	O	E	M	H	O	T	E	L	B
R	T	R	Y	R	H	M	E	V	L	R
V	F	T	X	C	O	X	T	G	A	E
K	A	Z	C	W	S	N	A	S	A	A
N	A	P	A	R	T	M	E	N	T	K
J	O	G	B	X	E	Q	M	R	B	F
K	P	E	I	O	L	T	X	S	C	A
R	M	V	N	A	A	R	V	N	A	S
O	U	H	O	H	I	D	G	Y	S	T

1 This can be a problem in the rain. __________
2 A place where young people normally stay. __________
3 You can drive with your bed in this! __________
4 A small country house. __________
5 You can drive this. __________
6 You only stay here to sleep and eat in the morning. __________
7 This is in a building, often in a city. __________
8 An expensive one has five stars. __________
9 A ski or beach vacation destination. __________

GRAMMAR IN ACTION

3 Complete the conversation with the correct form of *will* or *won't*. Use the verbs in parentheses.

Wall | Find friends | Chat

IAN
1 __________ (we / sleep) in tents?

GUIDE
No, you 2 __________ (not sleep) in a tent. You 3 __________ (stay) in a resort. Every night, we 4 __________ (cook) dinner over a campfire.

IAN
Sounds fun. What activities 5 __________ (we / do)?

GUIDE
You 6 __________ (go) walking and climbing in the mountains. We 7 __________ (teach) you how to read a map, so you 8 __________ (not get) lost. It 9 __________ (be) fantastic. You 10 __________ (not forget) the experience, I'm sure!

4 Complete the email with the present continuous form of the verbs in parentheses.

Hi Sonia,

What 1 __________ (you / do) this summer? In July, my parents 2 __________ (work), so Paul and I 3 __________ (not plan) anything special. He 4 __________ (go) to a soccer camp, and I 5 __________ (stay) with my grandparents. Then in August we 6 __________ (fly) to Mexico for a family vacation. My parents 7 __________ (rent) an apartment at the beach, and then we 8 __________ (drive) up to the mountains in a camper. I'm very excited!

5 Write sentences about the pictures. Use the correct form of *be going to* and the phrases in the box.

climb a mountain	get on a plane	go horseback riding
play volleyball	sleep in a tent	walk in the forest

1 He ____________________

2 She ____________________

3 He ____________________

4 She ____________________

5 They ____________________

6 They ____________________

CUMULATIVE GRAMMAR

6 Complete the text with the missing words. Circle the correct options.

I had [1] ____________ amazing vacation of my life last year. [2] ____________ go? I went to Peru on [3] ____________ adventure vacation! We built a shelter to sleep in and learned [4] ____________ new things, like how to catch fish and find fruit to eat in the forest. We played [5] ____________ sports, too. They were fun! I loved [6] ____________ kayaking, but I [7] ____________ horseback riding. It was frightening! I have a lot of photos. Would you like to see [8] ____________?

This vacation was [9] ____________ than my vacation two years ago. Now I [10] ____________ a lot of new friends. At the moment, we [11] ____________ emails to each other to get together this year. I can't [12] ____________!

1	a the more	b most	c the most
2	a Where did I	b What I did	c When did I
3	a some	b a	c an
4	a much	b a lot	c a lot of
5	a an	b any	c some
6	a going	b go	c do
7	a wasn't enjoy	b didn't enjoy	c not enjoy
8	a them	b they	c it
9	a better	b the best	c good
10	a has	b had	c have
11	a writing	b 're writing	c write
12	a to wait	b wait	c waiting

EXAM TIPS: Reading Skills

Reading: Multiple Matching

You will read three short texts about three different people.
They are all about the same topic. The title tells you what the topic is. There are seven questions.
To answer the question, you need to choose the correct answer, A, B, or C.

Example:

	Tim	*Tom*	*Ted*
Which person did a lot of sports at school?	*A*	*B*	*C*

Exam Guide: Multiple Matching

- Start by reading the title of the text so you know what the topic is.
- Read all the questions carefully and underline the important words. This helps when you look for the same information in the texts.

  Example:

  Which person did a lot of sports at school?
- Now read the three texts for the first time without stopping. Maybe you see information similar to the questions, but read to the end.
- Now read the first question again. Then look at the texts to find which person says this. Maybe you remember something from one of the texts, so go to that text first to check. If not, just read from the beginning until you find what you need.
- When you find the correct answer, underline the words in the text with the same meaning as the question. Write the number of the question next to the part you underlined. Then choose your answer, A, B, or C.

  Example:

  When I was a teenager, I was on the school hockey, track and field, and swimming teams.
- Then read the next question and do the same until you finish.
- You don't lose points for a wrong answer, so always choose a letter, even if you're not sure.

REMEMBER!

When you look for the answer, remember that the words in the question are probably different from the words in the text, but the meaning is the same. So if you see a word in the text that is the same as a word in the question, it is not automatically the correct answer.

Example:

I played a lot of sports after school when I was younger.

This is **NOT** the correct answer to the example question because the meaning is different from the question.

Reading Practice: Multiple Matching

1 **Underline the most important words in these questions.**

1 Which person does a lot of sports on the weekend?

Which person ...

2 loves trying new activities after school?

3 has a lot of online friends?

4 reads science and nature magazines on the Internet?

5 wants to study art or drama at school next year?

6 doesn't have any aunts, uncles, or cousins?

7 doesn't like living in a big city?

Tip! Underlining the most important words in the questions helps you to remember the information you need to find in the text.

2 **Match words 1–10 with their opposites in the box.**

after	boring	difficult	evening	finish	good	hate	late	short	~~small~~

1 big small

2 easy ______

3 early ______

4 love ______

5 long ______

6 start ______

7 before ______

8 morning ______

9 fun ______

10 bad ______

Tip! When reading the text, look for words or phrases that are opposites (often with a negative verb), or synonyms of the words in the question.

3 **Read the text and match the words in bold with the synonyms (1–9).**

One place on my **road** that's very popular with **young people** is the skate park. Some of my friends spend all their free time there. There is also a **big** gym near me, with some good **courses**, like swimming and dancing. **Many** of my friends **tell me** they would like to go there, too, but the **price** is too high. I **travel** to a cheaper gym, but it's not very near my house and so it's **difficult** to get to.

1 street road

2 a lot ______

3 large ______

4 say ______

5 teenagers ______

6 hard ______

7 go ______

8 cost ______

9 classes ______

4 **Choose the option, A or B, that has the same meaning as the question.**

0 Which person has a lot of homework to do?

(A) I spend about two hours every night on school work.

B In my school, the teachers don't usually give us much homework.

1 Which person isn't happy about their hair color?

A I have red hair, but I don't mind. It's the same as Ed Sheeran's!

B Everyone in my family has blond hair. It's boring. I want to be different.

2 Which person reads information about science on the Internet?

A There is so much interesting stuff to read online these days, especially science articles.

B I love reading my dad's science magazines. He buys them every month.

3 Which person doesn't mind getting up early in the morning?

A I have to get up at seven so I'm not late for school, but that isn't a problem.

B I'm glad when it's Saturday and I can get up late.

4 Which person thinks living in the country is boring?

A People say that the country is boring, but I think there's a lot to do.

B I'm happy I live in the city. I'm sure it's more exciting than being in a small town.

EXAM TIPS: Writing Skills

Writing: A Short Email or Note

You will write a short email or note of 25 words or more. The instructions in the test tell you exactly what you need to do.

Example:

You want to ***go to the movies*** *with* ***your friend*** *Jan on* ***Saturday****. Write an email to Jan.*

The instructions also explain three things you need to include in the text. For example:

In the email:

- **ask** Jan to **go to the movies** with you
- say **what movie** you want to see
- say **where** you can **meet.**

Exam Guide: Writing a Short Email or Note

- Read the instructions carefully and decide what kind of message is required.
- It is important to include all the points from the instructions in the text. It is also better to keep them in the same order as in the instructions.
- The text needs
  - an opening sentence
  - three sentences, one for each point
  - a sentence to close (for example a question asking your friend's opinion)
  - (in an email) your name at the end.
- When you finish, read the text again and count the number of words. If you have included all the information from the plan above, the text should be at least 25 words. If it's more, that's OK. If you haven't written 25 words, go back and check that you have included all the points and the opening and the closing sentences.

Writing: A Short Story

You will write a short story of 35 words or more. To help you there are three pictures. You write the story they show.

Exam Guide: Writing a Short Story

- Don't start writing immediately. Look at the pictures for a minute and decide what the story is about. A good way to plan a story is to think about *Who? Where? When?* and *What?*
- Give any people in the picture a name. Then write any useful vocabulary you want to use (nouns, verbs, adjectives, etc.) next to each picture.
- Decide how to start (e.g., *One day/Yesterday*). Use the past tense when you write your story.
- When you finish writing, count the words. You need to write at least 35 words.

REMEMBER!

You will receive a piece of paper to write notes or a draft. Use it to plan your writing.

Writing Practice: An Email or Note; a Short Story

1 Match the phrases from a text message with the right category A–C.

> **Tip!** Try to use different phrases for inviting and suggesting ideas.

A opening B inviting or suggesting C closing phrase

1 I'd like to see the new X-Men movie. B
2 What do you think? ______
3 Do you want to go swimming this afternoon? ______
4 Let me know soon. ______
5 Hey ______
6 Can we meet at the bus stop at seven? ______
7 Hi, Jan ______
8 We can try the new pool. ______
9 How about going to the movies on Saturday? ______

2 Order the words to make sentences from an email.

1 cheap / to / a / go / restaurant / Let's / . Let's go to a cheap restaurant.
2 want / during / Do / break / to / you / meet / the / ?
______
3 for / Why / days / we / don't / go / a few / camping / ?
______
4 what / know / Let / you / me / think / .
______
5 Tania / Hi / ,
______
6 climbing / I'd / go / again / to / like / .
______
7 my / can / tent / take / We / brother's / .
______

3 Separate the text into words and sentences. Then rewrite the email with the correct format and punctuation in your notebook.

> **Tip!** Always check your writing for spelling or punctuation.

heyjosedoyouwanttohangouttogetheronsaturdaywecangotothe newshoppingmallcanlicometoyourhouseatfourletmeknowsooncarlos

Hey José,

4 Correct the spelling of these words.

1 swiming swimming
2 shoping ______
3 wich ______
4 tenis ______
5 Wenesday ______
6 tomorow ______
7 bycicle ______
8 diferent ______
9 scool ______
10 begining ______

5 Put the words in the box in the correct place in the story.

> **Tip!** Use time words like *yesterday*, *after*, and *then* to make the order of events clear. Use words like *but* and *so* to show how the events connect.

After but so Then ~~Yesterday~~

[0] Yesterday Annie had a technology presentation at school, [1] ______ she got up late. [2] ______ she got to school, she saw her notes weren't in her bag. They were important, [3] ______ she called her dad and asked him to look for them. He found them in her room. [4] ______ he brought her notes to school. She was very happy.

EXAM TIPS: Listening Skills

Listening: Three-Option Multiple Choice

You will listen to five short texts. You will hear the text twice. Each text is about something different, and the question usually explains who is speaking, who they are speaking to, and what they are talking about.

Example:

You will hear ***two friends*** *talking about* ***their plans for the weekend.***

You then have to answer a question about each text, with three options, A, B, and C.

Example:

You will hear two friends talking about their plans for the weekend. ***What do they both plan to do?***

A They are ***both going*** *to a* ***basketball game.***

B They are ***both visiting*** *their* ***grandparents.***

C They are ***both going shopping*** *with* ***friends.***

You can write your answers on the question paper.

Exam Guide: Three-Option Multiple Choice

- Read the questions before you listen. Read the questions carefully because they tell you what to listen for.
- Underline the important words in the question. In the example, the most important word in the question is **both**.

  Example:

  What do they both plan to do?

  A They are both going to a basketball game.

  B They are both visiting their grandparents.

  C They are both going shopping with friends.

- When you listen the first time, try to decide what the correct answer is and circle A, B, or C. If you're not sure, don't worry. The second time you listen, you can check your first answer or decide for the first time.
- Sometimes the first time you listen, you hear that one answer is definitely wrong. Cross it out. Then the second time you listen, just focus on the other two possible answers.
- Always give an answer, even if you don't know which one is correct. You don't lose points for a wrong answer.
- When you have heard one text twice, don't spend a lot of time thinking about it. Focus on the next listening text when it starts.

REMEMBER!

You will usually hear the people talk about all the possible answers in some way, but this is a "trap." Only one answer is correct.

To avoid traps, listen carefully to every word. You will hear negative verbs (for example: *I'm not visiting my grandparents this weekend*) or things which are similar but not the same as the correct answer (for example: *I'm going shopping with my sister on Saturday*).

Listening Practice: Three-Option Multiple Choice

1 E.01 **Listen to the sentences. Mark (✓) if they are affirmative or (✗) if they are negative.**

1 ______ 2 ______ 3 ______ 4 ______ 5 ______ 6 ______

2 E.02 **Is the meaning of the sentences you hear the same as sentences 1–6? Write *Y* (yes) or *N* (no).**

1 I decided not to buy the shirt because I didn't like the color. ______
2 It takes Martin a quarter of an hour to walk home. ______
3 It was sunny yesterday. ______
4 Martin is flying to Spain on vacation. ______
5 Paula's sister has dark hair. ______
6 The teacher tells Eric to do his homework again. ______

3 E.03 **Read sentences 1–6. Then listen and correct the information that is different.**

1 Alex went to Scotland by bus last year. ______
2 Laia is going to stay in a hotel with her grandparents. ______
3 Donna usually goes to the bowling alley on the weekend. ______
4 Harry's mom lost her bus pass yesterday. ______
5 Last week, Megan saw a show about bears on TV. ______
6 Tom has a basketball game on Saturday morning. ______

4 E.04 **Listen and choose the correct option, A or B. You will hear each text twice.**

1 The teacher has a problem with Sarah's homework because …
  A she made a lot of mistakes.
  B she did the wrong page.
2 What's the weather like today?
  A It's cold and wet.
  B It's cloudy and warm.
3 What did Corrin and Vanessa do today?
  A They went out for a meal.
  B They went out with school friends.
4 How did Nico get home after the concert?
  A He caught the last bus.
  B His friend's dad gave him a ride.
5 What did Ollie buy at the shopping mall?
  A a new gym bag
  B some new sweatpants
6 What does Chloe's mother want her to do?
  A go shopping
  B clean her room

Subject Pronouns

Singul	Plural
I	we
you	you
he / she / it	they

- We use a subject pronoun before a verb.
  She is Brazilian. (NOT ~~*Is Brazilian*~~.)
- The singular and plural form of ***you*** is the same.

Possessive Adjectives

Singular	Plural
my	our
your	your
his / her / its	their

- We use possessive adjectives to show that something belongs to somebody. We always use possessive adjectives with a noun.
  Our house is big. *Their school is fun.*

Verb *To Be*

Affirmative	Negative
I'm Mexican.	I'm not Mexican.
You're Mexican.	You aren't Mexican.
He's / She's / It's Mexican.	He / She / It isn't Mexican.
We're Mexican.	We aren't Mexican.
You're Mexican.	You aren't Mexican.
They're Mexican.	They aren't Mexican.

Questions	Short Answers	
	Affirmative	Negative
Am I Mexican?	Yes, I am.	No, I'm not.
Are you Mexican?	Yes, you are.	No, you aren't.
Is he / she / it Mexican?	Yes, he / she / it is.	No, he / she / it isn't.
Are we Mexican?	Yes, we are.	No we aren't.
Are you Mexican?	Yes, you are.	No, you aren't.
Are they Mexican?	Yes, they are.	No, they aren't.

- We use **verb *to be*** to identify or describe something.
  They're red. *He's Spanish.* *It's good.*
- We usually use contractions in conversation.
  We're from Canada. *She's ten.*
- We change the word order in questions; we put ***to be*** before the subject.
  Is David OK? *Are you from London?*
  (NOT ~~*You are from London*~~?)
- We usually reply with short answers.
  A: *Is it blue?* ***B:*** *Yes, it is.* ***A:*** *Is it red?* ***B:*** *No, it isn't.*

Question Words

- We use ***what*** to ask for information.
  What is your favorite color?
- We use ***where*** to ask about places.
  Where are you from?
- We use ***when*** to ask about time.
  When is your birthday?
- We use ***how old*** to ask about age.
  How old is your father?
- We use ***who*** to ask about people.
  Who is your best friend?

Whose + Possessive Pronouns

	Singular	Plural
Whose book is this?	It's mine.	It's ours.
	It's yours.	It's yours.
	It's his / hers.	It's theirs.

- ***Whose*** asks about possession or ownership.
- We often use possessive pronouns to answer ***whose*** questions. They help us to avoid repeating information.
  Whose pencil is this? It's mine. (instead of *It's my pencil.*)
  We don't use ***its*** as a possessive pronoun.
  Whose book is this? (NOT ~~*It's its*~~.)
- We use ***this*** (singular) and ***these*** (plural) to talk about things that are near.
  This is my pencil. *These are my books.*
- We use ***that*** (singular) and ***those*** (plural) to talk about things that are not near.
  That is my bag. *Those are my pens.*

Imperatives

Affirmative	Negative
Stand up!	Don't stand up!
Open the book!	Don't open the book!

- We use the imperative to give orders or instructions.
  Come here, please.
- We use ***don't*** to form the negative.
  Don't write in your textbook.

GRAMMAR PRACTICE

Subject Pronouns and Possessive Adjectives

1 Complete the sentences with the correct subject pronouns and possessive adjectives.

1 My best friend Maria is from Paris. __She__'s French. __Her__ house is very big!

2 My name's Pablo. ________'m from Ecuador. I'm in ________ classroom.

3 Berat and Ahmet are Turkish. ________'re from Istanbul. These are ________ books.

4 My English teacher is Mr. Jones. ________'s from New York. ________ classes are fun!

5 Susie, ________'re my friend! Today is ________ birthday! Happy birthday!

Verb *To Be*

2 (Circle) the correct form of the verb *to be*.

Hi, my name [1](*is*) / *are* Alicia. My favorite color [2]*is* / *are* blue. I [3]*are* / *am* 12 years old. My best friends [4]*is* / *are* Laura and Eva. They [5]*isn't* / *aren't* from Mexico like me. They are from China. We [6]*is* / *are* in school today.

3 Match questions 1–6 with answers a–f.

1 Are you hungry?	d	a	Yes, we are.
2 Is your school big?		b	No, she isn't.
3 Is he in the room?		c	No, it isn't.
4 Is she from China?		d	~~Yes, I am!~~
5 Are we 12 years old?		e	No, they aren't.
6 Are they Canadian?		f	Yes, he is.

Question Words

4 Complete the conversation with the words in the box.

How old	When	~~Where~~	Who

A: Hi, Mateo. [1]__Where__ are you from?
B: I'm from Argentina.
A: [2]________ are you?
B: I'm 13.
A: [3]________'s your birthday?
B: It's in February.
A: [4]________'s your favorite singer?
B: Taylor Swift. She's great!

Whose + Possessive Pronouns

5 Write the words in the correct order to make questions. Then complete the answers with the correct possessive pronouns.

1 book / is / Whose / this /?
Whose book is this?
It's my book. It's __mine.__.

2 is / this / Whose / dictionary / ?
____
It's your dictionary. It's ________.

3 calculator / is / Whose / that / ?
____
It's his calculator. It's ________.

4 these / pens / Whose / are / ?
____
They're her pens. They're ________.

5 notebooks / those / are / Whose / ?
____
They're our notebooks. They're ________.

6 desks / are / Whose / those / ?
____
They're their desks. They're ________.

Imperatives

6 Write the affirmative or the negative.

1 Write on the paper.
Don't write on the paper.

2 ________________
Don't use your calculator.

3 Use your dictionary.
____

4 ________________
Don't listen to your teacher.

5 Close the door.
____

6 ________________
Don't do your homework.

GRAMMAR REFERENCE

To Have: Affirmative and Negative

Affirmative		Negative	
I have	short hair.	I don't have	brown eyes.
You have		You don't have	
He / She / It has		He / She / It doesn't have	
We have		We don't have	
You have		You don't have	
They have		They don't have	

- We use ***have*** to talk about possession.
  I have five cousins. *She has 12 grandchildren.*
- To make the negative, we put ***don't* / *doesn't*** before ***have***.
  We don't have a big house.
  She doesn't have a sister.

Possessive *'s*

Singular Nouns	Plural Nouns	Irregular Plural Nouns
Beth's computer	His parents' house	The women's soccer team
Carlos's bike	The students' books	The children's favorite toy

- We use **apostrophe + *s*** to indicate possession.
  This is Andrea's notebook.
- We put ***'s*** after a singular name or noun and ***s'*** after a plural name or noun.
  Carla's phone (NOT ~~*The phone of Carla*~~)
  His grandparents' house (NOT ~~*The house of his grandparents*~~)
- Some plural nouns are irregular. To show possession, we add ***'s***.
  men's, people's, children's
- When two people possess something, we use ***'s*** after the second noun.
  Paul and Amy's family
  Mom and Dad's computer

To Have: Questions

Question		Short Answers	
		Affirmative	Negative
Do	I have a blue book? you have a blue book? we have a blue book? you have a blue book? they have a blue book?	Yes, I do. Yes, you do. Yes, we do. Yes, you do. Yes, they do.	No, I don't. No, you don't. No, we don't. No, you don't. No, they don't.
Does	he / she / it have a blue book?	Yes, he / she / it does.	No, he / she / it doesn't.

- We use ***do*** + **subject** + ***have*** + **object** in questions.
  Do you have a bike? *Does your mom have a cousin?*
- In spoken English, we reply to questions with short answers.
  A: *Do you have a brother?*
  B: *Yes, I do.* (NOT *Yes, I do* ~~*have*~~*.*) / *No, I don't.* (NOT *No, I don't* ~~*have*~~*.*)

How Many ... Do You Have?

- We use ***how many*** + **object** + ***do*** + **subject** + ***have*** in questions to ask about the number of things.
  A: *How many cousins does he have?* **B:** *He has 30.*
  A: *How many brothers and sisters do you have?* **B:** *I have two sisters. I don't have a brother.*

GRAMMAR PRACTICE

To Have: Affirmative and Negative

1 Complete the sentences with the correct affirmative form of *to have*.

1 I ___have___ a dictionary.
2 We ______ six red pens.
3 My aunt ______ three sisters.
4 Mom and Dad ______ a mobile home.
5 You ______ 12 cousins.
6 Our house ______ five bedrooms.

2 Write the sentences in the negative.

1 I have two brothers.
I don't have two brothers.
2 We have a new teacher at school.
______
3 My grandma has ten grandchildren.
______
4 My best friends have green uniforms.
______
5 He has a bike.
______
6 We have a big house.
______

3 Look at the chart and complete the text with the correct form of *to have*.

	Javier	Rosa
sisters	1	2
brothers	0	1
cousins	2	2
bike	1	0
computer	0	0

Javier [1] ___has___ one sister; her name is Cecilia. He [2] ______ any brothers. He [3] ______ a blue bike. Rosa [4] ______ two sisters and one brother. She [5] ______ a bike. Javier and Rosa [6] ______ two cousins. They [7] ______ a computer.

Possessive *'s*

4 Write *s'* or *'s* in the correct places in the sentences.

1 My ~~dad~~ bike is gray and my ~~uncle~~ bike is black.
dad's *and my uncle's*
2 Natalia favorite color is green and her sister is blue.
______
3 His grandparent house is big, but his parent house is small.
______
4 Myra family are from India, and Diego family are from Spain.
______
5 Vero and Isaac English books are red. Their mom book is yellow.
______

To Have: Questions

5 Write the words in the correct order to make questions. Then match them with answers a–e.

1 have / I / Do / book / an / English / ?
Do I have an English book? ___*d*___
2 bike / a / Do / blue / have / you / ?
______ ______
3 pets / Alex / Does / two / have / ?
______ ______
4 Catalina / brother / have / a / Does / ?
______ ______
5 big / have / house / Do / they / a / ?
______ ______

a Yes, he does. He has two cats.
b No, she doesn't. She has a sister.
c Yes, they do.
~~d Yes, you do.~~
e No, I don't. It's green.

How Many … Do You Have?

6 Write questions with *How many* for the answers.

1 *How many cousins do you have?*
I have three cousins.
2 ______
My mom has two nephews.
3 ______
We have 20 teachers at our school.
4 ______
My best friend has two sisters.
5 ______
We have four subjects on Friday.

Simple Present: Affirmative and Negative

Affirmative	
I live	in Lima.
You live	
He / She / It lives	
We / You / They live	
Negative	
I don't live	in Lima.
You don't live	
He / She / It doesn't live	
We / You / They don't live	

- We use the simple present to talk about facts, habits, and routines.
  I speak Chinese. *He goes to school.*
  They study English.
- We form the negative of the simple present with the **subject** + ***don't*** / ***doesn't*** + **infinitive**.
  They don't speak English.
- We use ***doesn't*** in the third person (*he* / *she* / *it*).
  He doesn't do his homework.

Spelling: Third Person

- The third person form (*he* / *she* / *it*) of the simple present ends in **-*s***.
  eat – he eats *read – she reads*
- With verbs ending in **consonant** + ***y***, we replace the ***y*** with **-*ies*** for the *he* / *she* / *it* forms.
  study – she studies
- The *he* / *she* / *it* form of verbs ending in **-*ss***, **-*sh***, **-*ch***, **-*x***, and **-*o*** is **-*es***.
  kiss – she kisses *relax – he relaxes*
  finish – he finishes *go – she goes*
  teach – she teaches
- Some verbs have an irregular spelling in the third person.
  have – she has *be – he is*

Adverbs of Frequency

never — sometimes — often — usually — always
0% ⟵⟶ 100%

- Adverbs of frequency say how often we do something. They go after the verb *to be* but before all other verbs.
  She's always happy. *He sometimes checks his phone in the afternoons.*
  We usually do homework after school.
- With ***never***, we always use an affirmative verb.
  I never go out with my friends on Monday.
- In questions, adverbs of frequency always come after the subject.
  Do you always have English class on Wednesday?

Simple Present: Questions

Questions		Short Answers	
		Affirmative	Negative
Do	I like oranges? you like oranges?	Yes, I do. Yes, you do.	No, I don't. No, you don't.
Does	he / she / it like oranges?	Yes, he / she / it does.	No, he / she / it doesn't.
Do	we like oranges? you like oranges? they like oranges?	Yes, we do. Yes, you do. Yes, they do.	No, we don't. No, you don't. No, they don't.

- We form simple present ***Yes/No*** questions with ***do/does*** + **subject** + **infinitive**.
  Do you brush your teeth in the morning? Does she go to bed at 9 p.m.?
- We use short answers with ***do/does***. We don't repeat the main verb.
  A: *Do you often go to school by car?* ***B:*** *Yes, I do.*
  A: *Does he live in London?* ***B:*** *No, he doesn't.*

Wh- Questions

Question Word	*Do/Does*	Subject	Verb
Who	do	you	live (with)?
What time	does	the party	start?
Where	does	she	live?
What	does	his dad	do?
When	do	they	play?

- We form ***Wh-*** questions with a **question word** + ***do/does*** + **subject** + **verb**.
  What time do you go to bed? (NOT ~~*What time you go to bed*~~?)
  Where does he go to school?
- We also use the question ***How often … ?*** to ask about frequency.
  How often do you play video games?

Simple Present: Affirmative and Negative

1 Write the words in the correct order to make sentences.

1 I / every / day / wake / up / at / 7 p.m.
I wake up at 7 p.m. every day.

2 gets / up / takes / a / Antonio / shower / when / he
______

3 have / homework / Isa / Mondays / doesn't / on
______

4 don't / brothers / My / at / 8:30 p.m. / to / bed / go
______

5 lunch / school / We / have / at
______

6 my / with / homework / helps / My / dad / me
______

2 Complete the text with the simple present form of the verbs in parentheses.

On Saturday mornings, Chloe [1] gets up (get up) at 9 a.m. She [2] ______ (take) a shower and [3] ______ (brush) her teeth. Then she [4] ______ (get dressed) and [5] ______ (have) her favorite breakfast: toast and fruit juice. She [6] ______ (not see) her dad on Saturday mornings because he [7] ______ (go) to work.

At 10 a.m., she [8] ______ (go) to see her best friends, Grace and Ella. They [9] ______ (not live) near Chloe. She [10] ______ (go) on the bus to see them. Chloe [11] ______ (stay) at their house for about two hours. Then she [12] ______ (get) the bus to her grandma's house. She [13] ______ (visit) her grandma on Saturdays because she [14] ______ (not see) her during the week.

Adverbs of Frequency

3 Circle the correct options.

1 I ____ early in the morning.
(a) usually get up b get up usually

2 I ____ sports on the weekend.
a play often b often play

3 I ____ lunch with my sister at school.
a sometimes have b have sometimes

4 I ____ my homework in the evening.
a do always b always do

5 I ____ burgers for dinner.
a never eat b eat never

Simple Present: Questions

4 Complete the questions and answers. Use the verbs in parentheses.

1 Do you play tennis on the weekend? (play)
No, I don't.

2 ______ your cousin ______ to your school? (go)
Yes, he ______! He's in my class.

3 ______ your parents ______ Spanish? (speak)
No, they ______.

4 ______ you often ______ your phone? (check)
Yes, I ______.

5 ______ your aunt ______ in the United States? (live)
No, she ______.

6 ______ your sister ______ her school uniform? (like)
Yes, she ______.

Wh- Questions

5 Complete the questions with the words in the box.

How often	What	What time	~~When~~	Where	Who

1 When do you go to school?
2 ______ do your aunt and uncle live?
3 ______ does your dad do?
4 ______ do you walk to school with?
5 ______ do you have exams at school?
6 ______ does your mom get up?

6 Match the answers (a–f) with the questions in Exercise 5.

a My best friend. 4
b From Monday to Friday. ____
c In front of my house! ____
d Every month! ____
e He's an English teacher! ____
f At seven o'clock during the week and eight o'clock on the weekend. ____

GRAMMAR REFERENCE UNIT 3

Can for Ability and Permission

Affirmative		Negative	
I	can play the piano.	I	can't play the piano.
You		You	
He / She / It		He / She / It	
We		We	
You		You	
They		They	

- We use ***can*** to express ability or permission.
  He can play the guitar. (ability)
  Dad says we can play video games tonight. (permission)
- ***Can*** is the same in all forms. The *he/she/it* form doesn't end in ***-s***.
  She can speak Portuguese.
- We always use the infinitive without ***to*** after ***can***.
  They can go to school.
  (NOT ~~They can to go to school~~.)

Can: Questions

Yes/No Questions	Short Answers	
	Affirmative	Negative
Can I go?	Yes, I can.	No, I can't.
Can you go?	Yes, you can.	No, you can't.
Can he / she / it go?	Yes, he / she / it can.	No, he / she / it can't.
Can we go?	Yes, we can.	No, we can't.
Can you go?	Yes, you can.	No, you can't.
Can they go?	Yes, they can.	No, they can't.

- We change the word order when we form questions. We don't use ***do/does***.
  Can you use your dictionary at school?
  (NOT ~~*Do you can use your dictionary at school*~~?)
- We use the adverbs ***very well***, ***well***, ***quite well***, ***not very well***, ***badly***, or ***not at all*** to describe how we are able to do things.
  A: *Can you play the guitar?* **B:** *Yes, but not very well.*

Verb Forms: *(Don't) Like, Don't Mind, Love, Hate + -ing*

- We use the ***-ing*** form of the verb after ***like***, ***don't like***, ***don't mind***, ***love***, and ***hate***.
  She loves reading books. (NOT *She loves ~~read~~ books.*)
  I don't mind going to school. (NOT *I don't mind ~~go~~ to school.*)
- We can also use nouns after these verbs.
  They don't mind geography, but they love history.

Object Pronouns

Subject Pronoun	I	you	he	she	it	we	you	they
Object Pronoun	me	you	him	her	it	us	you	them

- We use object pronouns after some verbs and prepositions.
  She meets my sister and me after school every day. – She meets us after school every day.
  I usually have lunch with my friends. – I usually have lunch with them.
- For animals and things, we use ***it*** (singular) and ***them*** (plural).
  Don't feed the bird! – Don't feed it!
  Do you read books? – Do you read them?
- We can also put an object pronoun after ***like***, ***don't like***, ***don't mind***, ***love***, and ***hate***.
  This is my new book. Do you like it? (NOT ~~*Do you like*~~?)
  I don't like Mondays. I hate them.

GRAMMAR PRACTICE

UNIT 3

Can for Ability and Permission

1 Write sentences with *can*. Then write *A* (ability) or *P* (permission).

1 Daniel / sing / very well
Daniel can sing very well. ______ A
2 My dad / speak / French
______ ______
3 I / use / my dad's / computer / in the evening
______ ______
4 My brother / dance / well
______ ______
5 Harry / play / the guitar well
______ ______
6 You / use my / phone
______ ______

2 Change the sentences in Exercise 1 to the negative.

1 Daniel can't sing very well.
2 ______
3 ______
4 ______
5 ______
6 ______

Can: Questions

3 Look at the chart and write questions and answers about Alberto and Sara.

	Alberto	Sara
take good photos	✔	✘
paint well	✘	✔
dance salsa	✔	✘

1 Can Alberto take good photos? ______ Yes, he can.
2 ______ ______
3 ______ ______
4 ______ ______
5 ______ ______
6 ______ ______

Verb Forms: (*Don't*) *Like*, *Don't Mind*, *Love*, *Hate* + *-ing*

4 Complete the text with the words in parentheses.

My sister [1] loves going (love / go) to school.
She [2] ______ (like / study). I'm different!
I [3] ______ (love / see) my friends at school.
I [4] ______ (not mind / learn) new things,
but I [5] ______ (not like / take) exams and
I [6] ______ (hate / get up) early every day!

Object Pronouns

5 Match questions 1–5 with answers a–e. Then circle the correct object pronouns.

1 Do you like listening to your teacher? ______ b
2 Does your brother talk a lot? ______
3 Do you love hanging out with your friends? ______
4 Can your friends help you and your sister? ______
5 Do you always go to judo classes? ______

a Yes, he does, but I don't listen to *it* / *him*.
b Yes, I love listening to *me* / *her*.
c Yes, and my cousin comes to classes with *him* / *me*.
d Yes, I do. I meet *them* / *it* every day.
e No, they can't help *us* / *you*.

6 Rewrite the sentences with the object pronouns in the box.

her him it them ~~them~~ us

1 I like hanging out with my friends.
I like hanging out with them.
2 I can't find my pen.
______
3 I like my aunt.
______
4 They can't see you or me.
______
5 I love chatting online with my cousin, David!
______
6 I visit my grandparents on Sundays.
______

GRAMMAR REFERENCE

Countable and Uncountable Nouns

- Countable nouns can be counted individually. They have a singular and a plural form.
  one apple – two apples *one book – three books*
- Uncountable nouns can't be counted individually. They don't have a plural and are always singular.
  bread (NOT ~~*a bread*~~) *milk* (NOT ~~*a milk*~~) *homework* (NOT ~~*a homework*~~) *music* (NOT ~~*a music*~~)

A/An, Some/Any

	Singular Countable	Plural Countable	Uncountable
Affirmative	I have an orange.	I have some tomatoes.	I have some chocolate.
Negative	I don't have an orange.	I don't have any tomatoes.	I don't have any chocolate.
Question	Do you have an orange?	Do you have any tomatoes?	Do you have any chocolate?

- We use ***a*** with singular countable nouns.
  a banana *a cat* *a snack*
- We use ***an*** with singular countable nouns when the noun starts with a vowel sound.
  an orange *an uncle*
- We use ***some*** and ***any*** when we don't know a quantity or it's not important.
- We use ***some*** and ***any*** with plural countable nouns. ***Some*** is usually used in affirmative sentences and ***any*** in negative sentences and questions.
  We need some apples. *He doesn't have any tomatoes.* *Do we have any carrots?*
- We also use ***some*** and ***any*** with uncountable nouns. ***Some*** is usually used in affirmative sentences, and ***any*** in negative sentences and questions.
  We need some juice. *Marta doesn't have any water.* *Do we have any rice?*

There Is/Isn't, There Are/Aren't

	Singular	Plural
Affirmative	There's a quiz today.	There are some eggs on the table.
Negative	There isn't a quiz today.	There aren't any eggs on the table.
Questions	Is there a quiz today?	Are there any eggs on the table?
Short Answers	Yes, there is. No, there isn't.	Yes, there are. No, there aren't.

- We use ***there is*** with singular countable and uncountable nouns.
  There is a school.
  There is some cheese. (NOT *There ~~are~~ some cheese.*)
- We use ***there are*** with plural countable nouns.
  There are some potatoes. *There are four pizzas.*
- In questions and negatives we usually use ***any*** with plural countable and uncountable nouns.
  Are there any bananas? *Is there any milk?*
  There aren't any burgers. *There isn't any bread.*
- In informal English we can use the contraction ***there's***, but we don't use a contraction for ***there are***.

Much/Many, A Lot Of

	Countable Plural	Uncountable
Affirmative	There are a lot of eggs.	There's a lot of cheese.
Negative	There aren't many eggs.	There isn't much cheese.
Questions	How many eggs are there?	How much cheese is there?

- We use ***much***, ***many***, and ***a lot of*** to express quantity.
- We use ***much*** in negative sentences with uncountable nouns.
  There isn't much water.
- We use ***many*** in negative sentences with countable nouns.
  There aren't many tomatoes.
- We use ***a lot of*** in affirmative sentences with plural countable and uncountable nouns to describe a big quantity of something.
  There are a lot of vegetables. *We have a lot of rice.*
- We use ***how many*** with plural countable nouns and ***how much*** with uncountable nouns to ask about quantity.
  How many carrots are there? *How much juice do you have?*

GRAMMAR PRACTICE

UNIT 4

Countable and Uncountable Nouns

1 Circle the correct options.

1 I have an (apple) / *oranges* in my bag.
2 Alba has some *potato* / *meat* for lunch.
3 I have a *banana* / *bread*.
4 He doesn't have an *cheese* / *egg* for breakfast.
5 We don't have any *chocolate* / *carrot*.
6 They have some *pear* / *milk*.

A/An, Some/Any

2 Complete the sentences with *a*, *an*, *some*, or *any*.

1 We need ___some___ milk and ___some___ eggs.
2 I have ________ apple and ________ cheese for lunch.
3 Do you have ________ oranges, Mom? I want to make ________ orange juice.
4 We can't make a cake! We don't have ________ eggs!
5 I want to make a sandwich. I need ________ tomato and ________ egg.
6 Let's buy ________ bottle of soda and ________ fruit at the supermarket.

There Is/Isn't, There Are/Aren't

3 Complete the conversation with the correct form of *there is* / *there are*.

A: Let's make a salad!
B: [1] ___Are there___ any tomatoes?
A: Yes, [2] ____________, but [3] ____________ any onions.
B: OK, that's not a problem. [4] ____________ some cheese, and [5] ____________ ten carrots.
A: I don't want ten carrots in my salad! Let's make spaghetti!
B: Sorry! [6] ____________ any pasta!

4 Write sentences about the food and drink words in the box. Use the correct form of *there is* / *there are* and *some* or *any*.

apples ✔ bread ✘ carrots ✔ eggs ✘ water ✔ bananas ✘

1 ___There are some apples.___
2 ____________
3 ____________
4 ____________
5 ____________
6 ____________

Much/Many, A Lot Of

5 Circle the correct options. Then match questions 1–5 with answers a–f.

1 How (much) / *many* fruit do you eat every day? [e]
2 How *much* / *many* people are there in your family? [ ]
3 Do you spend *much* / *many* time checking your phone? [ ]
4 How *many* / *much* snacks do you have every day? [ ]
5 How *much* / *many* water do you drink at home? [ ]
6 Are there *much* / *many* bottles of soda in your fridge? [ ]

a There are seven: I have a lot of brothers and sisters!
b About two liters a day – more if I play tennis.
c There aren't any. We only drink water and milk at home.
d No! I don't have much time to look at it!
e ~~I eat an apple every morning~~.
f I don't eat any! I'm too busy.

Present Continuous: Affirmative and Negative

Affirmative		Negative	
I'm	eating dinner.	I'm not	eating dinner.
You're		You're not	
He's / She's / It's		He's / She's / It's not	
We're		We're not	
You're		You're not	
They're		They're not	

- We use the present continuous to talk about actions in progress at the time of speaking.
  You are reading this sentence.
- For the affirmative, we use **subject** + ***to be*** + **verb** + ***-ing***.
  The dog is sleeping. *The children are playing.*
- For the negative, we put ***not*** after ***to be***.
  She is not (isn't) downloading songs.

Present Continuous: Questions

(Question Word)	*To Be*	Subject	Verb + *-ing*
-	Am	I	reading?
-	Are	you	thinking?
-	Is	he / she / it	sleeping?
-	Are	we / you / they	learning?
What	are	you	doing?
Where	is	she	going?

Short Answers	
Affirmative	**Negative**
Yes, I am.	No, I'm not.
Yes, you are.	No, you aren't.
Yes, he / she / it is.	No, he / she / it isn't.
Yes, we / you / they are.	No, we / you / they aren't.

- To form questions, we use ***to be*** + **subject** + **verb** + ***-ing***.
  Are you listening?
- We don't use the **verb** + ***-ing*** in short answers.
  Yes, I am. (NOT *Yes, I am ~~listening~~.*)
- We form information questions with the ***Wh-*** question word before *be*.
  Who are you talking to? *What are they doing?*

Spelling: *-ing* Form

- With most verbs, we add ***-ing*** to the infinitive.
  eat – eating *read – reading* *think – thinking*
- For verbs ending in ***-e***, we remove the ***-e*** and add ***-ing***.
  write – writing *have – having* *give – giving*
- For verbs ending in a vowel and a consonant, we double the final consonant and add ***-ing***.
  stop – stopping *shop – shopping*
  plan – planning

Simple Present and Present Continuous

- We use the simple present to talk about facts, habits, and routines.
  Red and yellow make orange.
  I read a lot of books.
  He usually wears boots.
- We use the present continuous to talk about actions in progress at the time of speaking.
  I read a lot of books. At the moment, I'm reading a really good one.
  He usually wears boots, but he's wearing sneakers today.
- Some verbs are not usually used in the continuous form: ***hate***, ***know***, ***like***, ***love***, ***need***, ***remember***, ***think***, ***understand***, ***want***.
  I like that song. (NOT *I'm ~~liking~~ that song.*)
- We use expressions like ***at the moment*** and ***right now*** with the present continuous.
  He's playing video games at the moment.

GRAMMAR PRACTICE

UNIT 5

Present Continuous: Affirmative and Negative

1 Write the *-ing* form of the verbs.

1 eat ___eating___
2 write ______
3 chat ______
4 play ______
5 swim ______
6 have ______

2 Complete the sentences with the present continuous form of the verbs in the box.

chat	get dressed	have	listen	~~read~~	use

1 Luis ___is reading___ a book.
2 My grandparents ______ their dinner.
3 The teacher ______ to our stories.
4 My mom ______ to go to a party this evening.
5 You ______ my computer in school today.
6 I ______ with my friends online.

3 Rewrite the sentences in Exercise 2 in the negative form of the present continuous. Use contractions.

1 Luis isn't reading a book.
2 ______
3 ______
4 ______
5 ______
6 ______

Present Continuous: Questions

4 Complete the questions with the present continuous form of the verbs in parentheses. Then write the short answers.

1 ___Are___ you ___doing___ (do) your homework?
Yes, ___I am___.
2 ______ your sister ______ (read) a book?
No, ______.
3 ______ your uncle ______ (make) dinner?
Yes, ______.
4 ______ we ______ (have) sandwiches for lunch?
No, ______.
5 ______ my grandparents ______ (watch) TV?
No, ______.
6 ______ the cat ______ (sleep) on my bed?
Yes, ______.

Simple Present and Present Continuous

5 Complete the rules. Write *present continuous* or *simple present.*

1 To talk about facts, routines, and habits, we use the ______.
2 To talk about an action in progress at the time of speaking, we use the ______.
3 We use *always, often, usually, sometimes,* and *never* with the ______.
4 We use *right now* and *at the moment* with the ______.

6 Circle the correct options.

My name is Carolina. At the moment, I'm on vacation and I [1]*help* / *'m helping* my dad. We have a big yard, and he usually [2]*works* / *is working* all the time, so he's tired on the weekend. Now he is on vacation, too. I [3]*like* / *'m liking* flowers, and we usually [4]*collect* / *are collecting* some to put in the house. Right now, my dad [5]*paints* / *is painting* the fence and, of course, my brother [6]*watches* / *is watching* us do all the work!

Comparatives

Comparatives	
Short Adjectives *smart*	add *-er*: *smarter*
Short Adjectives Ending in Vowel + Consonant *big*	double the final consonant and add *-er*: *bigger*
Adjectives Ending in -*e* *safe*	add -*r*: *safer*
Adjectives Ending in -*y* *easy*	remove the -*y* and add -***ier***: *easier*
Long Adjectives *interesting*	put ***more*** before the adjective: *more interesting*
Irregular Adjectives *good* *bad*	 *better* *worse*

- We use comparative adjectives to compare one thing with another. We use the **verb *to be*** + **a comparative adjective** + ***than***.
  Daniel is taller than his father.

Superlatives

Superlatives	
Short Adjectives *smart*	add -***est*** *smartest*
Short Adjectives Ending in Vowel + Consonant *big*	double the final consonant and add -***est***: *biggest*
Adjectives Ending in -*e* *safe*	add -***est***: *safest*
Adjectives Ending in -*y* *easy*	remove the -*y* and add -***iest***: *easiest*
Long Adjectives *interesting*	put ***most*** before the adjective: *most interesting*
Irregular Adjectives *good* *bad*	 *best* *worst*

- We use superlative adjectives to say a thing or person has the most of a particular quality. We use ***the*** with a **superlative adjective**.
  Daniel is the tallest person in his family.

GRAMMAR PRACTICE

UNIT 6

Comparatives

1 Match the adjectives with their opposites.

1 big [d]
2 boring [ ]
3 easy [ ]
4 tall [ ]
5 old [ ]
6 healthy [ ]

a unhealthy
b short
c new
d ~~small~~
e difficult
f interesting

2 Write the comparative form of the adjectives in the box next to the comparative with the same spelling rule.

bad comfortable heavy nice ~~old~~ thin

1 smarter *older*
2 bigger ______
3 safer ______
4 easier ______
5 more interesting ______
6 better ______

3 Write sentences with comparatives about Amy's family.

1 my sister / short / me
My sister is shorter than me.

2 my brother / young / me
______

3 my sister / funny / my brother
______

4 my mom / thin / my dad
______

5 my brother / old / my sister
______

6 my / cousin / intelligent / me
______

Superlatives

4 Complete the chart with the superlative.

Adjective	Comparative	Superlative
high	higher	1 *the highest*
amazing	more amazing	2 ______
easy	easier	3 ______
bad	worse	4 ______
popular	more popular	5 ______
big	bigger	6 ______

5 Complete the sentences with the superlative form of the adjectives in parentheses.

1 I think my dad is the *best* (good) dad in the world.

2 Many soccer players are the ______ (rich) people in sports.

3 My mom says Formula 1 racing is the ______ (fast) sport.

4 This is the ______ (heavy) bag in the world! What do you have in it?

5 I think hockey is one of the ______ (dangerous) sports.

6 Which is the ______ (easy) sport to learn?

6 Complete the text with the comparative or superlative form of the adjectives in parentheses.

On Saturdays, I usually go and see my cousin play soccer. She's [1] *the best* (good) player on the team. She always scores [2] ______ (amazing) goals! She's [3] ______ (tall) player on the team, and she's [4] ______ (fast) than the others. I think she's also [5] ______ (intelligent) than her teammates because she watches what is happening all the time! She's also [6] ______ (popular) player on the team!

GRAMMAR REFERENCE

UNIT 7

Simple Past: *To Be*

Affirmative		Negative	
I / He / She / It	was good.	I / He / She / It	wasn't good.
You / We / They	were good.	You / We / They	weren't good.

Questions	Short Answers	
	Affirmative	Negative
Was I / he / she / it good?	Yes, I / he / she / it was.	No, I / he / she / it wasn't.
Were you / we / they good?	Yes, you / we / they were.	No, you / we / they weren't.

- ***Was*** and ***were*** are the simple past forms of ***to be***.
  There was a special gorilla in the Barcelona zoo.
  The elephants were born without tusks.
- To form questions, we use ***was/were***. We don't use ***do***.
  Was he a white tiger? (NOT ~~*Does he was a white tiger*~~*?*)
  Were the elephants enormous?
- We form information questions with the ***Wh-*** question before ***was/were***.
  What was it? *Where were you last night?*

There Was/Were

	Affirmative	Negative
Singular	There was a gorilla at the zoo.	There wasn't a gorilla at the zoo.
Plural	There were three lions.	There weren't three lions.

Questions	Short Answers	
	Affirmative	Negative
Was there a gorilla at the zoo?	Yes, there was.	No, there wasn't.
Were there three lions?	Yes, there were.	No, there weren't.

- ***There was/were*** are the simple past forms of ***there is/are***.
  There was a park here. *There were two cars.*
- We use ***there was*** with singular countable nouns and uncountable nouns.
  There was a pen here. *There was some milk in the fridge.*
- We use ***there were*** with plural countable nouns.
  There were a lot of tourists in our town last weekend.
- In questions and negatives, we usually use ***any*** with plural countable and uncountable nouns
  Were there any interesting animals at the zoo?
  Was there any bread at home?
  There weren't any cats. *There wasn't any rice.*

Simple Past: Regular and Irregular Verbs

- We use the simple past to talk about completed events and actions in the past.
  I played basketball yesterday.
  He lived in Boston last year.

Spelling

Most Verbs	add ***-ed***: *show – showed*
Verbs Ending in *-e*	add ***-d***: *live – lived*
Verbs Ending in Consonant + *-y*	remove the ***-y*** and add ***-ied***: *study – studied*
Verbs Ending in Consonant + Vowel + Consonant	double the final consonant and add ***-ed***: *shop – shopped* *stop – stopped*

Irregular Verbs

- Irregular simple past verbs don't follow any pattern.
  get – got *do – did* *see – saw* *have – had*

Simple Past: Negative

	Didn't	Infinitive	Other Words
I / You / He / She / It / You / We / They	didn't	play	soccer yesterday.
		go	to the movies.

- To form the simple past negative, we use **subject + *didn't* + infinitive.**
  Javier didn't watch TV last night.
  They didn't have lunch at home today.
- We can use time expressions such as ***yesterday***, ***last night***, ***last weekend***, and ***last summer*** with the simple past. We usually put them at the end of a sentence.
  We went to a safari park last weekend.
- We use ***ago*** with the simple past to talk about when something happened. We usually put it at the end of a sentence.
  Alex arrived home two hours ago.

GRAMMAR PRACTICE

UNIT 7

Simple Past: *To Be*

1 Circle the correct options.

1 The monkey was / *were* in a tree at the zoo.

2 The baby elephant *was / were* beautiful!

3 The bears *wasn't / weren't* very big, but the lions *was / were* enormous!

4 It *wasn't / weren't* a very interesting documentary – it *was / were* very boring!

5 We *was / were* at the zoo for hours!

6 Lalo *was / were* happy, but Emilia *wasn't / weren't*!

2 Put the words in the correct order to make questions. Then complete the answers with *was* or *were*.

1 happy / Lisa / was / ?

A: Was Lisa happy?

B: Yes, she was.

2 yesterday / were / Where / you / ?

A: ____________________

B: I ________ at home.

3 were / Who / with / you / ?

A: ____________________

B: My friend ________ at home with me.

4 the / zoo / Was / big / ?

A: ____________________

B: Yes, it ________ enormous!

5 most / What / animal / was / the / interesting / ?

A: ____________________

B: The tigers! They ________ beautiful.

There Was/Were

3 Circle the correct options.

For many years, [1]*there wasn't* / there weren't many people in my town, and [2]*there wasn't / there weren't* a place to see animals, but in 2015, everything changed – [3]*there was / there were* houses, people, children, and stores, and [4]*there was / there were* a new animal park! [5]*There wasn't / There weren't* any big animals, like elephants, but [6]*there was / there were* cute little animals, like rabbits and a lot of different birds. Now, it's my favorite place!

Simple Past: Regular and Irregular Verbs

4 Write the simple past form of the verbs in the chart.

Regular	watch	live	hate
	1 watched	5 ________	9 ________
	plan	stop	study
	2 ________	6 ________	10 ________
Irregular	do	eat	get
	3 ________	7 ________	11 ________
	go	have	see
	4 ________	8 ________	12 ________

5 Complete the text with the simple past form of the verbs in parentheses.

We [1] arrived (arrive) at the animal park in the morning. My little sister [2] ________ (want) to see the birds, but they were at the other end of the park. She [3] ________ (cry) for a few minutes. Then I [4] ________ (show) her the rabbits. She [5] ________ (love) them! She [6] ________ (play) with them for hours!

6 Write the words in the correct order to make sentences.

1 week / my / went / to / dad / mountains / Last / I / the / with

Last week, I went to the mountains with my dad.

2 brown / bears / saw / big / We / two

____

3 so / we / had / My / dad / a sandwich / was / hungry,

____

4 behind / I / bear / me / heard / a

____

5 up / a / tree, / I / went / bear / ate / my / sandwich / and / the

____

6 My / the / ran / to / car / eat / his / sandwich, but / dad / didn't

____

Simple Past: Questions

Did	Subject	Infinitive	Short Answers	
			Affirmative	Negative
Did	I / you / he / she / it / we / you / they	play?	Yes, I / you / he / she / it / we / you / they did.	No, I / you / he / she / it / we / you / they didn't.

- We make simple past questions with ***Did*** + **subject** + **the infinitive**.
  Did she enjoy the yoga class?

Simple Past: *Wh-* Questions

Question Word	*Did*	Subject	Verb	Other Words
Who	did	I / you / he / she / it / we / you / they	go	with?
What time				?
Where				?
What				for?
When				?
How				?

- We form ***Wh-*** questions in the simple past with a **question word** + ***did*** + **subject** + **the infinitive**.
  What time did you go to bed?
  Where did they go on vacation?
  What did you do on the weekend?
  Who did she see there?
  How did he feel?
  When did you arrive?

GRAMMAR PRACTICE

UNIT 8

Simple Past: Questions

1 Match questions 1–5 with answers a–e.

1 Did you go to the post office this morning? [d]
2 Did you and Antonia watch TV last night? [ ]
3 Did the store close early yesterday? [ ]
4 Did your friends go to the bowling alley with you? [ ]
5 Did our English teacher correct our homework? [ ]

a No, she didn't.
b Yes, we did.
c Yes, they did.
d ~~Yes, I did~~.
e No, it didn't.

2 Look at the information about the activities Sergio and Andrea did on the weekend. Write short answers.

	Go Bowling	Clean Bedroom	Visit Grandparents	Go Swimming
Sergio	✓	✗	✓	✗
Andrea	✗	✓	✓	✗

1 Did Sergio go bowling? *Yes, he did.*
2 Did Sergio clean his bedroom? ________
3 Did Andrea clean her bedroom? ________
4 Did Sergio visit his grandparents? ________
5 Did Andrea go swimming? ________
6 Did Sergio go swimming? ________

3 Write questions and short answers.

1 your cousins / see / the fish / at the / aquarium ✓
A: *Did your cousins see the fish at the aquarium?*
B: *Yes, they did.*

2 Daniel / go to / the skate park / yesterday ✗
A: ________
B: ________

3 you and Melody / meet / at the movies / today ✓
A: ________
B: ________

4 Olga / do / judo / last year ✗
A: ________
B: ________

5 you / stay / at the hospital / for a long time ✓
A: ________
B: ________

Simple Past: *Wh-* Questions

4 Circle the correct options.

1 A: *What* (circled) / *Where* did you do on the weekend?
B: I stayed at home.

2 A: *Where* / *When* did they play handball on Sunday?
B: At the gym.

3 A: *What* / *Who* did he see at the ice rink?
B: Nobody he knew.

4 A: *How* / *When* did he feel?
B: Not very well.

5 A: *How* / *What* time did they leave?
B: About 5 p.m.

6 A: *When* / *Who* did they catch the train?
B: Early this morning.

5 Complete the conversation with *Wh-* question words from Exercise 4.

Eduardo: I like your phone. [1] *Where* did you get it?
Ali: It's from the new shopping mall.
Eduardo: Was it expensive?
Ali: I don't know! It was a present.
Eduardo: [2] ________ bought it for you?
Ali: My mom. She got it for my birthday!
Eduardo: Wow, that's a fantastic present! [3] ________ did she get it?
Ali: She got it last week when we went shopping, but I didn't see her buy it!
Eduardo: [4] ________ did you feel when you got it?
Ali: Surprised and happy!
Eduardo: [5] ________ did I get you? I can't remember!
Ali: Nothing, you forgot!
Eduardo: Sorry!

Future with *Will/Won't*

Affirmative		Negative		Questions		Short Answers	
						Affirmative	Negative
I/You/He/ She/It/We / You/They	will pass the exam.	I/You/He/ She/It/We / You/They	won't pass the exam.	Will I/you/ he/she/it/ we/you/they	pass the exam?	Yes, I/you/ he/she/it/ we/you/they will.	No, I/you/ he/she/it/ we/you/they won't.

- We use ***will*** and ***won't*** to make predictions about the future.
  Computers will control our lives in the future.
- ***Will/Won't*** doesn't change in the third person.
- We change the word order when we form questions. We don't use ***do/does***.
  Will we travel in cars in the future?
- In informal English, we use the contraction ***'ll***.
  They'll sleep in a camper on vacation.

Present Continuous for Future

- We can use the present continuous to talk about fixed arrangements in the future.
  I'm meeting my friend Maite at 6:30.
  My sister's traveling to Brazil in October.
- We often use future time expressions such as ***tonight***, ***tomorrow***, ***this weekend***, ***this summer***, ***next week***, ***next month***, and ***after class/school***.
  What are you doing tonight?
  We're traveling to Paris this summer.
  Is he coming to the party on Saturday?

Be Going To

Affirmative		Negative	
I'm	going to run.	I'm not	going to run.
You're		You aren't	
He's		He isn't	
She's		She isn't	
It's		It isn't	
We're		We aren't	
You're		You aren't	
They're		They aren't	

- We use ***to be going to*** to talk about future plans and intentions.
  She's going to take her camera on vacation.
  I'm going to wear my new sneakers.
- To form the affirmative, we use **verb *to be*** + ***going to*** + **infinitive**.
  We're going to have dinner in a restaurant.
- To form the negative, we use **verb *to be*** + ***not*** + ***going to*** + **verb infinitive**. ***Not*** is usually contracted.
  They aren't going to go on vacation this summer.

Questions	Short Answers	
	Affirmative	Negative
Am I going to be there?	Yes, I am.	No, I'm not.
Are you going to be there?	Yes, you are.	No, you aren't.
Is he going to be there?	Yes, he is.	No, he isn't.
Is she going to be there?	Yes, she is.	No, she isn't.
Is it going to be there?	Yes, it is.	No, it isn't.
Are we going to be there?	Yes, we are.	No, we aren't.
Are you going to be there?	Yes, you are.	No, you aren't.
Are they going to be there?	Yes, they are.	No, they aren't.

- We form questions with **verb *to be*** before the subject.
  Is he going to tell us the answers to the homework?
- We form information questions with a ***Wh-*** question word before **verb *to be***.
  Who is he going to ask?
  What are you going to wear to the party?
  Why is Susana going to be late?

GRAMMAR PRACTICE

Future with *Will/Won't*

1 Complete the sentences about a camping trip. Write *'ll* or *won't*.

1 Don't sit at the bottom of the boat. You 'll ________ get wet.
2 Don't make the shelter. You ________ know how to do it.
3 Don't swim in the river. It's dangerous, so you ________ be safe!
4 Don't eat and then swim. You ________ feel sick!
5 Don't walk alone at night because you ________ get lost!
6 Don't lose your compass. You ________ know how to get back to the camp.

2 Write sentences with *will* or *won't* about the things you can do on vacation.

1 have a good time ✓ I will have a good time.
2 get bored ✗ ________
3 go to the beach every day ✓ ________
4 stay in a tent ✗ ________
5 eat good food ✓ ________
6 do any homework ✗ ________

Present Continuous for Future

3 Complete the email with the present continuous form of the verbs in parentheses.

Hi Sandra,

How are you? It's summer break next week! I [1] 'm going (go) on an adventure trip, and my sister [2] ________ (come), too! In August, my dad [3] ________ (take) me on a boat trip! My mom [4] ________ (not go) because she doesn't like boats! She [5] ________ (visit) my grandparents. I think you [6] ________ (fly) to England for a week. Is that right? What are you doing after that?

Jorge

4 Complete the sentences with the present continuous form of the verbs in the box.

come	go	have	~~meet~~	not visit	play

1 I'm meeting my friends tomorrow morning.
2 When ________ you ________ basketball?
3 ________ grandpa ________ to visit on Sunday?
4 ________ Ben and Sam ________ a party next week?
5 We ________ my aunt and uncle this weekend.
6 Where ________ you ________ shopping on Friday?

Be Going To

5 Rewrite the sentences in the negative.

1 I'm going to see my grandma next week.
I'm not going to see my grandma next week.
2 You are going to make new friends.
____
3 Marina is going to visit the wildlife park next month.
____
4 Sam is going to go to a summer camp next year.
____
5 We are going to learn how to make a shelter.
____
6 They are going to climb the mountain.
____

6 Complete the conversations with the correct form of *be going to*. Use the verbs in parentheses.

1 A: What are you going to do (do) on summer break?
B: I ________ (visit) my aunt in Chicago.
2 A: ________ (he / stay) in a hotel?
B: No, he ________.
3 A: ________ (Gabriel and Ana / go) rock climbing in the mountains?
B: Yes, they ________.
4 A: We ________ (not go) on vacation this year.
B: ________ (you / stay) at home?

STARTER

Vocabulary

Months

January February March April May
June July August September
October November December

Cardinal Numbers

one two three four five
six seven eight nine ten

Ordinal Numbers

first second third fourth fifth sixth
seventh eighth ninth tenth

Colors

black blue green orange pink
red yellow white

Classroom Objects

board calculator chair dictionary
door notebook pen pencil poster
ruler table window

Grammar in Action

Subject Pronouns and
Possessive Adjectives
Verb *To Be*
Question Words
Whose + Possessive Pronouns
Imperatives

Writing

Useful Language

An Informal Letter

To start: Dear + Mr. (*man*) or Mrs./Ms. (*woman*) + person's surname

To end: Best wishes, Sincerely

To join two ideas in one sentence: and

UNIT 1

Vocabulary

Family Members

aunt brother cousin dad daughter
granddaughter grandma
grandpa grandson husband mom
nephew niece sister son uncle wife

Describing People

Eyes: brown, gray
Hairstyle: long, short, wavy
Hair Color: blond, brown, gray, red
Height: short, tall
Other features: beard, freckles, glasses, mustache

Grammar in Action

To Have: Affirmative and Negative
how many … ?
Possessive *'s*

Speaking

Everyday English

Are you alright?
Cool!
Gotta go!
That's funny!
That's so not funny!

Useful Language

Bye!
Hey, (Evan).
How's it going?
OK/Fine, thanks. You?
See you later.

Writing

Useful Language

An Informal Email

At the beginning: Hi, Hey, Hello

At the end: Email me soon, That's all for now, Write soon!

Contractions: I'm, He's, She's, We're, Here's, Who's

Symbols: use emojis to help express your feelings

LANGUAGE BANK

UNIT 2

Vocabulary

Daily Routines

brush your teeth | check your phone | do your homework | get dressed | get up | go home | go to bed | go to school | have breakfast | pack your bag | take a shower | wake up

Free-Time Activities

chat online | download songs | go for a bike ride | go shopping | hang out with friends | listen to music | make videos | play an instrument | play video games | read a book/magazine | take photos | watch TV

Grammar in Action

Simple Present: Affirmative and Negative
Adverbs of Frequency
Simple Present: Questions
Wh- Questions

Speaking

Everyday English

Go ahead.
It depends.
No problem.
Sure.
That's easy!

Useful Language

Is that OK?
Thank you very much for your time.
I just have some questions to ask you.
I just have one more question.
That's interesting.

Writing

Useful Language

An article

apostrophe **'**
comma **,**
capital letter **A**, **B**, **C**
exclamation point **!**
period **.**
question mark **?**

UNIT 3

Vocabulary

School Subjects

art | drama | English | geography | information technology (IT) | math | music | nutrition | physical education (PE) | science | Spanish | vocational education

Places in a School

athletic field | auditorium | cafeteria | classroom | computer lab | gymnasium | library | locker room | office | restrooms | science lab | teacher's lounge

Grammar in Action

Can for Ability and Permission
Verb Forms: *(Don't) Like*, *Don't Mind*, *Love*, *Hate* + *-ing*
Object Pronouns

Speaking

Everyday English

Don't be silly!
I'm stuck.
Not again!
Not great.
Oh, dear!

Useful Language

Are you sure?
Can you do me a favor?
Can you help me, please?
Do you need a hand with … ?

Writing

Useful Language

A Description

for example
like
such as

UNIT 4

Vocabulary

Food and Drink

apples bananas beans carrots cheese
chicken chocolate eggs fish
juice meat rice soda water

Adjectives

cold delicious disgusting fresh healthy
hot salty spicy sweet unhealthy

Grammar in Action

Countable and Uncountable Nouns
A/An, Some/Any
There Is/Isn't, There Are/Aren't
Much, Many, A Lot Of

Speaking

Everyday English

Enjoy!
Here you go.
No problem.
No worries.

Useful Language

Can I have … ?
Can I help you?
How much is that?
I'd like a/an/some …
Is that everything?
That's … , please.
What kind?
What's in the … ?

Writing

Useful Language

A Description

We use *and* to add similar information.
We use *but* to contrast different information.
We use *or* when there is a choice (usually between two things).

UNIT 5

Vocabulary

Clothes

boots cap flip-flops hoodie jacket
jeans shirt shorts
skirt sneakers sweatpants T-shirt

Accessories

belt bracelet earrings gloves necklace
purse ring scarf sunglasses umbrella
wallet watch

Grammar in Action

Present Continuous
Simple Present and Present Continuous

Speaking

Everyday English

It's a bargain.
It's perfect.
No, honestly.
You're in luck!

Useful Language

Can I help you?
Can I see the … one, please?
Do you have it in a different (size/color/style)?
How about this one / these?
I'm looking for …
It comes in …

Writing

Useful Language

A Description of a Photo

in the back
in the middle
on the left/right
next to (someone)

UNIT 6

Vocabulary

Sports

basketball football gymnastics
hockey rock climbing rugby running
sailing swimming table tennis
track and field volleyball windsurfing yoga

Sports Verbs

bounce catch climb dive hit jump
kick lift pass run score throw

Grammar in Action

Comparatives
Superlatives

Speaking

Everyday English

Got them!
Look!
That's crazy!
What are we waiting for?
Why not?

Useful Language

Do you want to go?
How much are the tickets?
Let's buy them.
Let's go.
They're ($145).
What's the (quickest/best/cheapest) way to get there?

Writing

Useful Language

A Profile of an Athlete

We use *also* and *too* to give extra information.
We use *also* after the verb *to be*.
We use *also* before other verbs.
We use *too* at the end of a sentence.
We use a comma before *too*.

UNIT 7

Vocabulary

Animals

Birds:
duck eagle parrot
Mammals:
bear donkey giraffe hippo horse
lion monkey mouse whale
Reptiles:
crocodile snake

Adjectives

beautiful cute dangerous heavy
huge large lazy light long noisy
quiet safe short smart tiny wild

Grammar in Action

Simple Past: *To Be, There Was/Were*
Simple Past: Regular and Irregular Verbs

Speaking

Everyday English

No way!
Really?
Wow!
You're joking!

Useful Language

How was (the field trip)?
It was (really cool).
What about (lions)?
What was (it) like?

Writing

Useful Language

An Article

In 2017
On October 10, 2015
Several years ago

LANGUAGE BANK

UNIT 8

Vocabulary

Places in Town

aquarium   bowling alley   gym   hospital
ice rink   movie theater   parking lot
post office   shopping mall   skate park
swimming pool

Personal Possessions

bus pass   camera   concert ticket   headphones
ID card   keys   laptop   money   passport
phone   portable charger   tablet

Grammar in Action

Simple Past: Questions
Simple Past: *Wh-* Questions

Speaking

Everyday English

Calm down.
Don't panic!
Gross!
Let's think.

Useful Language

Did you have it when you (got to school)?
Did you put it (in your bag)?
What did you do with it after that?
When did you last (have/use/see) it?

Writing

Useful Language

A Blog Post

I didn't hear my alarm, **so** I got up late.

UNIT 9

Vocabulary

Outdoor Life

build a shelter   catch fish   collect wood
cook over a campfire   find food and water
identify plants   light a fire   pick fruit
read a map   use a compass

Vacations

apartment   (beach/ski) resort
B&B (bed & breakfast)   cabin   camper   hotel
RV (recreational vehicle)   tent   youth hostel

Grammar in Action

Future with *Will/Won't*
Present Continuous for Future
Be Going To

Speaking

Everyday English

Easy!
Forget that.
I'm on it!
You're unbelievable!

Useful Language

How about a (movie night)?
I'm not sure about that.
I'd rather not do that.
Let's do that!
What are we going to do?
Why don't we (have a picnic)?

Writing

Useful Language

An Email

at home
in August
in the morning
on Monday
on August 3
at the airport

IRREGULAR VERBS

Infinitive	Simple Past
be	was/were
beat	beat
become	became
begin	began
break	broke
bring	brought
build	built
buy	bought
catch	caught
choose	chose
come	came
cost	cost
cut	cut
do	did
draw	drew
drink	drank
drive	drove
eat	ate
fall	fell
feel	felt
fight	fought
find	found
fly	flew
forget	forgot
get	got
give	gave
go	went
grow	grew
have	had
hear	heard
hide	hid
hit	hit
hold	held
keep	kept

Infinitive	Simple Past
know	knew
leave	left
lose	lost
make	made
meet	met
pay	paid
put	put
read	read
ride	rode
ring	rang
run	ran
say	said
see	saw
sell	sold
send	sent
show	showed
shut	shut
sing	sang
sit	sat
sleep	slept
speak	spoke
spend	spent
stand	stood
swim	swam
take	took
teach	taught
tell	told
think	thought
throw	threw
understand	understood
wake	woke
wear	wore
win	won
write	wrote

ACKNOWLEDGEMENTS

The authors and publishers acknowledge the following sources of copyright material and are grateful for the permissions granted. While every effort has been made, it has not always been possible to identify the sources of all the material used, or to trace all copyright holders. If any omissions are brought to our notice, we will be happy to include the appropriate acknowledgements on reprinting and in the next update to the digital edition, as applicable.

Key: **SU** = Starter Unit, **U** = Unit

Photography

The following photographs are sourced from Getty Images.

U1: Radius Images; kali9/iStock/Getty Images Plus; Carol Yepes/Moment; Classen Rafael/EyeEm; s-cphoto/E+; scibak/iStock/Getty Images Plus; RinoCdZ/iStock/Getty Images Plus; C Squared Studios/Photodisc; AigarsR/iStock/Getty Images Plus; abell7302/iStock/Getty Images Plus; Westend61; m-imagephotography; Tempura/iStock/Getty Images Plus; Rafael Elias/Moment; SSC/Stone; Xose Casal Photography/Moment; Jose Luis Pelaez Inc/Blend Images; Gustavo Di Mario/The Image Bank; Anders Johansson/EyeEm; Floresco Productions/Cultura; Andrew Bret Wallis/The Image Bank; jane/iStock/Getty Images Plus; Thomas Barwick/Taxi; Bruce Laurance/The Image Bank; aimintang/iStock/Getty Images Plus; Kalle Singer; Juanmonino/iStock/Getty Images Plus; ImagesBazaar; Simon D. Warren/Corbis/VCG; **U2:** bamby-bhamby/iStock/Getty Images Plus; Klaus Vedfelt/DigitalVision; JGI/Jamie Grill/Blend Images; instamatic/iStock/Getty Images Plus; SolStock/iStock/Getty Images Plus; SolStock/E+; Jim Jordan Photography/The Image Bank; James Collins/Corbis; Steve Debenport/E+; Glenda Christina/Perspectives; FatCamera/E+; Lobro78/iStock/Getty Images Plus; Westend61; Purestock; Robert Daly/Caiaimage; Morsa Images/DigitalVision; Jamie Grill/The Image Bank; JGI/Tom Grill/Blend Images; Juanmonino/iStock/Getty Images Plus; Nick David/Taxi/Getty Images Plus; **U3:** Jupiterimages/Stockbyte; YinYang/E+; Wavebreakmedia/iStock/Getty Images Plus; NikolayN/iStock/Getty Images Plus; uptonpark/iStock/Getty Images Plus; Klaus Vedfelt/Taxi; Jon Feingersh/Blend Images; Mint Images RF; Eri Morita/The Image Bank; Vanda9/iStock/Getty Images Plus; Compassionate Eye Foundation/London, United Kingdom; hartcreations/E+; Image Source; Dinodia Photo/Passage; Amos Morgan/Photodisc; alongoldsmith/RooM; B2M Productions/Photographer's Choice RF; **U4:** Dougal Waters/DigitalVision; Theerawan Bangpran/iStock/Getty Images Plus; Derkien/iStock/Getty Images Plus; Magone/iStock/Getty Images Plus; rimglow/iStock/Getty Images Plus; Foodcollection RF; tc397/iStock/Getty Images Plus; MielPhotos2008/iStock/Getty Images Plus; vanillaechoes/iStock/Getty Images Plus; chengyuzheng/iStock/Getty Images Plus; ddukang/iStock/Getty Images Plus; Onegin/iStock/Getty Images Plus; Bartosz Luczak/iStock/Getty Images Plus; Astrakan Images/Cultura; imtmphoto/iStock/Getty Images Plus; Vladimir Godnik; Donald Iain Smith/Blend Images; Buena Vista Images/DigitalVision; Veronika Lipar/EyeEm; Axel Bueckert/EyeEm; Karly Pope/Moment Open; Arx0nt/iStock/Getty Images Plus; LauriPatterson/E+; Teen00000/iStock/Getty Images Plus; Science Photo Library; IvanMikhaylov/iStock/Getty Images Plus; Simone_Capozzi/iStock/Getty Images Plus; joakimbkk/iStock/Getty Images Plus; Inmagineasia; **U5:** OxfordSquare/iStock/Getty Images Plus; s-cphoto/iStock/Getty Images Plus; primeimages/E+; mfto/iStock/Getty Images Plus; mawielobob/iStock/Getty Images Plus; akova/iStock/Getty Images Plus; traveler1116/iStock/Getty Images Plus; Bounce/Cultura; 3alexd/E+; macroworld/iStock/Getty Images Plus; Maskot; gradyreese/E+; FatCamera/iStock/Getty Images Plus; Richard Drury/DigitalVision; Jeremy Woodhouse/Blend Images; **U6:** omgimages/iStock/Getty Images Plus; FrankRamspott/iStock/Getty Images Plus; Sam Kadiri/EyeEm; Hermann Erber/LOOK-foto; Meinzahn/iStock/Getty Images Plus; bowdenimages/iStock/Getty Images Plus; Cultura Exclusive/Rebecca Nelson; David Rogers/Getty Images Sport; Patrik Giardino/Corbis; gbh007/iStock/Getty Images Plus; Erik Isakson/Blend Images; Will Gray/AWL Images; Dennis Grombkowski/Getty Images Sport; Ramin Burhani/EyeEm; Echo/Juice Images; Foto Olimpik/NurPhoto; Feng Li/Getty Images Sport; Markus Gann/EyeEm; Hero Images; Ty Allison/Photographer's Choice; lzf/iStock/Getty Images Plus; Tim Clayton - Corbis/Corbis Sport; skynesher/E+; **U7:** Dugwy/iStock/Getty Images Plus; GlobalP/iStock/Getty Images Plus; mtruchon/iStock/Getty Images Plus; Alexey_Seafarer/iStock/Getty Images Plus; reisegraf/iStock/Getty Images Plus; PAUL J. RICHARDS/AFP; Chasing Light - Photography by James Stone james-stone.com/Moment; ROGER HARRIS/Science Photo Library; CoreyFord/iStock/Getty Images Plus; kavram/iStock/Getty Images Plus; SharafMaksumov/iStock/Getty Images Plus; Jim Cumming/Moment; Sudowoodo/iStock/Getty Images Plus; MariaArefyeva/iStock/Getty Images Plus; Quim Roser/Cultura; COffe72/iStock/Getty Images Plus; PeopleImages/E+; Sean Fleming/EyeEm; CreativeNature_nl/iStock/Getty Images Plus; Mostafa Gabr/EyeEm; ERNESTO BENAVIDES/AFP; Barrie Thomas/EyeEm; Dave Fleetham/Design Pics/Perspectives; Anup Shah/Stockbyte; Dennis George Booth/EyeEm; Paul A. Souders/Corbis Documentary; Jeffrey Coolidge/DigitalVision; Janos/iStock/Getty Images Plus; Tim Platt/Stone; Danita Delimont/Gallo Images; baronvsp/iStock/Getty Images Plus; Mr_Khan/iStock/Getty Images Plus; jashlock/iStock/Getty Images Plus; **U8:** fotovampir/iStock/Getty Images Plus; lkpgfoto/iStock/Getty Images Plus; GOLFX/iStock/Getty Images Plus; Colin Anderson Productions pty ltd/DigitalVision; MandM_Photo/iStock/Getty Images Plus; Chalabala/iStock/Getty Images Plus; Weekend Images Inc/E+; PhotoAlto/Odilon Dimier/PhotoAlto Agency RF Collections; Fancy/Veer/Corbis/; bbostjan/E+; Westend61; farakos/iStock/Getty Images Plus; urbancow/E+; PBNJ Productions/Blend Images; Steve Woods Photography/Cultura; duncan1890/DigitalVision Vectors; gresei/iStock/Getty Images Plus; luismmolina/iStock/Getty Images Plus; Creative Crop/DigitalVision; rustemgurler/iStock/Getty Images Plus; Jamie Grill; Michael Burrell/iStock/Getty Images Plus; cudger/iStock/Getty Images Plus; Cahir Davitt/AWL Images; Ingolf Hatz/Cultura; Maremagnum/Photodisc; Ed Bock/Corbis; Jon Shireman/Photonica; Spaces Images/Blend Images; wakila/E+; ihoe/iStock/Getty Images Plus; kevinjeon00/E+; Vostok/Moment & Vostok/Moment; Perboge/iStock Editorial/Getty Images Plus; **U9:** Daft_Lion_Studio/iStock/Getty Images Plus; Zero Creatives/Cultura; GomezDavid/E+; Westend61; PeopleImages/E+; Don Mason/Blend Images; Ryan McVay/Photodisc; ewg3D/iStock/Getty Images Plus; jfoltyn/iStock/Getty Images Plus.

The following photographs are sourced from other library.

SU, U1, U3, U5, U8 & U9: Carboxylase/Shutterstock.

Illustration

SU, U3, U5, U6: Antonio Cuesta; **U1, U4, U5:** Jose Rubio; **U1, U5, U6:** Alex Herrerias.

Cover design and illustrations: Collaborate Agency

Audio Recordings: Eastern Sky Studios

American English Consultant: Cara Norris-Ramirez

Freelance Editors: Sue Costello, Suzanne Harris, Rebecca Raynes, and Gareth Vaughan